Exegesis of Lucifer

By

Richard K. Page

Editing By Diane Narraway

Forward

Welcome reader. Some years ago in my spiritual search for enlightenment into what is the real nature of our conscious existence, I found myself engaging into many Luciferian concepts. It seemed for the traveller, trying to pin down who or what Lucifer was, that we find ourselves lost in a deep sea of theological minefields. So many versions that it diluted out any remanence of a concept that I could happily accept and claim "Aha! This is Lucifer".

Is he a god, an angel, a devil, a demon, a serpent? Yet furthermore could he also have been Prometheus, a fallen angel, the creator of sin, a concept, an ideology? Was he Satan or was he even Jesus? I couldn't even pin down if he was male or female. All cases were argued to the point that it didn't make any sense.

By writing **Exegesis of Lucifer**, I endeavour to collate this can of worms into a single reference book, and disambiguate all these collective stories into one principle, to put them into a context that fits within my own greater Gnostic ideology. I hope to also provide a little background into the regions and cultures that created the icons we now Identify as aspects or interpretations of Lucifer.

I ask that you indulge me in the first couple of chapters, which I have used to expand on the concept of creation as told in Abrahamic hermetic texts; texts that lead for most people, to the origins of a Lucifer from a Hebrew if not earlier standpoint, through to the Roman pantheon, then through the

Greek biblical translations to the mismatch of information we have today which form the greater part of what is I suppose neo-Luciferianism.

I think then you will understand better my perceptions of the subject, rather than if I simply push out a series of abstract legends. I hope this preamble will be foundational in sharing my ambiguous collective thoughts on the matters.

This book is written in English. English as explained in ***Exploring the Divine*** is a remarkable language in that it is a bastard language. English is made up of historical influence, translation and accents from nearly all other languages on face of the Earth.

So by this it is comparable to the biblical language of tongues, prophesied as spoken by the angels. English is understood almost worldwide geographically, and though not <u>the</u> most spoken language by persons in number, it is by far the most globally widespread in number of countries. By speaking English all our words are rooted in other languages, there is very little if any Language that originated in these tiny islands that we can claim as being original English, as such we owe the world for our tongue. But to our advantage, with a little open mindedness this means we can easily see colorations in words that cross continents.

English complexity puts us in good stead to bridge the roots of words from their ancient foreign origins in ways that have been lost by modern complexities.

• • •

Let me give you an example that I have used often.

Think about the word "horizon" when we think of a horizon we see The Sun in the distance, a long horizontal plane of the earth, a sunset or sea scape.

"Horizontal", was mentioned as you can see, it's obvious when pointed out, the link is there, you subconsciously knew a clear link between the horizon and the word horizontal, but because we tend to use them relating to completely abstract purposes we possibly never had reason to merge the reference in the word horizon with the concept of horizontal unless you were a pilot or technical artist.

But let's take it a stage further, Horus one of the Egyptian gods of The Sun, in fact he is the son of Osiris also liked with The Sun, and brother of Set, the evil side of the Trilogy of Egyptian Sun gods. Not to mention Ra or Re.

In these Gods we have Horus-Son (Horizon) Sun-Set, Sun-Ra-ys. Our gods are also known as Deities, which can be written in short form, or as part of translation from other languages as 'deus', phonetically this also lends itself to 'day-isis' and you should know that Isis was in mythology the Mother character to Horus's.

Horus is an anagram of Hours, we have twenty-four hours in the day and we observe and record these solar and celestial events using terms such as degrees, which is the measure of an arc when I think about the phonetics of arc, we get Arc, Arch, Architecture, Archology, Arch-Angel, or Arch-Angle.

The ability to link these words is important in making your way through these subjects, shapes of letters, numbers and objects iconographically need to be flexible in your mind so that you can see the link.

You will I hope forgive me if when I wish to emphasise one of these abstract links, I simply place it in brackets behind the keyword, rather than explain each link, hopefully you can see it yourself, as many reoccur through-out the book.

The Sun is round and this creates a great O shape, Half of God in Greek is the Omega, the other half is the Alpha, the Greek word Omega literally translates to 'The Great O' or 'Big O' in the same way we say mega-store to mean a big store.

We steal language all the time, yet pay it little attention unless we are particularly interested in words and their origins, we are so familiar with our language, we often don't think about how these words came about.

But don't get caught up in spelling, you also have to allow for pronunciation and phonetics, even reading a book from 200 years ago you will see words spelled entirely different to the way we spell them today, Phonetics is key to your discovery here.

Radius for example is also used as a measure of area, its radiation, ra-deos, rodeos has a link to cattle, strangely and one of the themes of cattle is prevalent in astrological study, particularly bulls (balls,bells,baals (baal is a round, yet bulls are not)) please allow for ambiguity, it will all come together in the end.

Horses for example (Horus, Hours, Hairs (Horus is a line)) in a round ro-und stadium (stud-io). From Horus we can go to Chorus, Chords, Order all having musical influence in the words as we use them today.

IO (Eye Ow) is used to denote opposition, it is the line and the circle, the male and the female I is the male, O is the female for obvious reasons. The Sun rises in the I'st (east) male, risen (rizon) sun, born to Isis (eyes-eas) and sets in the O'st (west) female, in the eve'ning. We will go into this more later. You may have noticed the single quote splitting the word evening, this is to draw your attention to the character Eve from the bible. You will be amazed how many words we use are of this kind of intent in ancient texts.

I'm not suggesting all these are links as fact, some are clearly conjecture but please be open to these concepts as I will be using them a lot, but will always justify the ones I use.

Language evolves and like the evolutionary process in all scientific study, sometimes we have to make leaps of faith until further supporting evidence allows us to more fluidly connect things.

"Consider now, O reader! What trust can we place in the ancients, who tried to define what the Soul and Life are—which are beyond proof – whereas those things which can at any time be clearly known and proved by experience remained for many centuries unknown or falsely understood."

-Leonardo Da Vinci

Note* I would like to offer my apologies to those reading on e-book formats as I realise that text with pictures do not format very well on these devices and the picture layout in book form that I assure you is nicely laid out gets lost in digital format.

Contents

The Beginning of Time

Approximately fourteen billion years ago, if we concede that time is a consistently occurring phenomenon where a second is an equal division of one sixtieth of a minute, and that our method of observation which depicts the expansion of our known universe is also constantly aligned with that measurement. Then it is strongly theorised that there was a significant event, lovingly coined 'The Big Bang'. The event where it is assumed that all things were created, all matter, all space and all of time.

I feel a physical sense of awe when I try to conceive of what must have been before this event, this feeling is not exactly a pain, but it is a manifestation and a physical sensation of wonderment. As to conceive of what existed before those three base components of the universe came about, is simply overwhelming in a mind that knows no other state than its experienced state of existence. One of man's first steps into the metaphysical is imagining concepts outside of his personal life, where was I before conception and where will I be after death?

When we satisfy our subjective belief of these matters the philosophical will then proceed into a larger picture, what existed before the universe and what will be outside or after the universe if the universe is finite.

Everything that I can believe to be the state of existence is laid out before me in its current manifestation. The theorised alternate state of nothingness or 'the void' as it is called, is I believe genuinely inconceivable to any rational mind.

Surely to try to imagine the void brings you teetering on the edge of insanity, if you succeed in any part to grasp the infinite void then this very notion may be a precipis from which you may not return. With that in mind, I choose to imagine the void as somewhere I am not; it is a veil or bubble that forms the edge of reason and on the other side lies something I fear. I choose not to peer through but to simply allow my imagination to declare this place as the place beyond all.

If the empty void ever existed at all then even the mind itself on its most ethereal level, is still tangible and quantifiable, and therefore it defies the existence of such a void by its own presence. A void must be by nature void of all things.

If we are to accept that before matter, a conciousness or God existed within the void itself, then there was no void, and for conciousness to exist outside the void is also inconceivable, as what lies beyond the void cannot be another void. Likewise the borders of the universe cannot now still be contained within a void, as that would mean the void contained something (our universe) and therefore is no longer a void. So what is our universe contained in.

Whatever it may be, let us put this nonsense behind us and see if we can simply define our universe and its origins.

Picture for me please, the entire universe as a bubble floating in the 'void' and then mentally begin to resize it back into a single individual sphere maybe the size of a tennis ball. A ball, however made up of 'the stuff of the universe' shimmering and glittering like a Christmas scene snow globe or a magical scrying crystal ball. Within it you can see nebulas, galaxies and untold wonders, but this is just artistic license. Even at this scale our entire galaxy would be invisible to your naked eye as it would appear to be the size of an atom. No galaxies would be visible in fact, the universe would just be a black sphere, like polished obsidian, such is its vastness.

Now collapse it furthermore to the size of a pea, and surrounding it is an infinite void of nothing, the nothing is without colour, without shade and form, it is not black, nor is it white, but nothing, colourless and stateless. Already it gets difficult, what can we imagine if not blackness at the very least, but for the sake of our sanity, we will go with a void of grey.

Now shrink your universal snow globe from the pea, now even tinier than a single atom, then take away the concept of the measurement of time passing, while it is waiting for the big bang to occur; time after all is a construct to record and measure the change in state of the universe in increments, but I want to imagine what was before the big bang, in a prior to big bang state, there can be no change, so there is no time either, infinity and an instant are merged. This state also cannot be as time must have existed otherwise the change into creation could not have occurred.

For lack of a better description, the period or moment before time existed was both eternal and instantaneous combined. The universe was infinitesimally small but was infinitely large, and the largest thing in both existence and non-existence simultainiously, it was the quantum as yet undefined and that's only if you can even call something existent when time or any alternate state for a comparison equally do not exist, yet must exist.

We have the ultimate unity of ultimate duality, a contradiction of plausibilty. We have an example equal to the indestructable, unmovable block being hit by the indestructable, unstopable block.

We have the divine, the word divine means 'god like', and after all, God in the science of this must not exist in the void, and so if there ever was to be a god then it would be the first, last and all things created combined. The entirity of the universe would be God who then must create all of his dominion within himself and again the void could not be a void if a concience was contained within it.

All our science combined as yet will concur that there isn't really any such thing as creation. What we term and conveniently call 'created' is really a description of an entity or group of entities being transformed from one state in to another, and so this tiny snowglobe state of our universe prior to the big bang and being changed in to what it is now, is where we have come up with the first ever conceived 'Singularity' derived from the hypothetical sense of the word.

A singularity is a scientific term used to describe just such an infinitely small concept; a singularity is where time and matter are so closely condensed that they become one single indistinguishable entity. In this case, all our universe's energy, matter, space and time condensed into a single indivisible core unit.

It has been theorised that singularities exist in the centre of stars, black holes or galaxies, a point in space-time where forces combine to have infinite density and zero volume as observed from outside of the singularity.

Moreover, these are the stuff of infinite power, the cause that makes the universe expand and galaxies rotate, the momentum that causes all components within that vast expanse to be pulled or pushed or rotated. An energy that is so vast that it causes vibrations in nothingness so regular and consistent that they generate a force of resistance that we call solid objects. Matter is simply energy acting as a force defining itself as a physical shape for the absorption, reflection and refraction of other energies.

So not only were time, matter and all space contained within this one and only singularity, we now can only conclude that all things created in our (as we perceive it now) known universe were once a part of that singularity, every atom in your body, all the world, The Sun, all the other stars, all animals and even all the space in between them, plus all the events that occurred in the measurement of time that has already passed between then and now and all the things that will happen in the future, going on forever were all already contained in that single entity.

Isn't that just incredible?

If we then expand on that, with an obvious leap of conjecture, and while I'm sure you would come to similar conclusion without my prompting, but in order to steer you down the path which I want to lead you, we are a significant part of that entity both then and now.

We are all, for all intents and purposes, a physical, yet partially independent component of this eternal, infinite universe. We are made up of that self-same insubstantial energy exhibiting itself as matter, but incredibly that we are matter with an independent consciousness not only separates man from beasts, but separates us from 99.99…(keep going for almost ever with more nines)% of the rest of the universe. That's how special we are. We have self-awareness, we are 'special matter' and by that special attribute alone we are already as gods in an otherwise mindless yet exotic universe. Despite all this we are still one of the many components that make up the universe as an entity within itself. What I mean is, even though we are 'semi-independent' we actually are the universe or at least a small part of it.

A popular saying I believe accredited to Carl Sagan is 'We are the universe experiencing itself', and this has profound resonance when we really ponder the implications of such a statement.

To relate this to oneself, look at your hands and think 'my hand is a part of me'. You can cut it off (not that I am suggesting you do) but it is still a part of 'you'. Your hair, eyes, legs are all a part of you, rather than individual constituents they are slightly more integral.

Now getting a bit more morbid and macabre, imagine your death or more significantly your corpse, now let's say you donated your body to the wonderful exhibition 'Bodies' by Gunther von Hagens which uses human donation to exhibit the human form in the anatomical sense. If you have not seen it, please do look it up it's quite an experience. And for the purpose of the exhibition you were to be dismembered, but as a ghostly observer to your dissection you watch yourself being chopped up into lots of pieces, is there any point where they stop being you? To you and your observation no. To you they will eternally be 'my hand' or 'my leg' because they are linked observationally to you by your psycological bonding agent 'your spirit', to an external observer they would be 'a hand' or 'a leg' and to someone that has formed a semblance of relationship to you they may even be 'your arm' or 'your leg' because their spirit has formed an emotional bond with you be it long term or simply for the period of a brief encounter.

I threw 'Spirit' into that sentence a bit early without actually defining my concept of your spirit, but in brief, the only thing 'you' can separate from your physical body and imagine as a separate element is your consciousness or spirit, your 'stuff of life' if you will.

It is quite possible to conceive taking your brain, putting it into another body, and it would still be 'you' don't you think?

What if we then take it a step further, and instead of the physical brain we simply had a way of transferring not only your memory but your consciousness into another body, is it still you?

We are now no longer talking about any physical part of you, we are talking about your ethereal individualism which despite being unique to you is as best we can tell common in its physical makeup yet some measurement of 'stuff' separates you from others.

For a period of time you may see your old body, laying on the table as the 'you' that has been the physical definition of 'you' for all your life, and separating this vessel from the long-held definition of who you are will take some time, but after occupying your new host body for a while, and looking back on your body like in the stories of 'outer body experiences' would you then still see your old body as 'you' or merely a vessel for which your consciousness could swim through the space between other material objects.

I believe, given a relatively small time in your new host body, the spirit would define that host as you and your old body would be superfluous, a nostalgic memory but nothing more, we are very adaptable spirits.

So we now have two distinct definitions of what constitutes you; the physical body used as a vehicle that is secondary but significant to the spiritual or consciousness elements that truly define you.

The word consciousness itself has two similar but distinct definitions, one is the medical state of consciousness, being awake or alert and the other type of consciousness which is the one I will be referring to throughout this book, the ethereal or spiritual components that make up our individuality and personality.

Adaptation is a mechanism built into our spirit that forms our current self. We learn as we go that this constantly changes who we are. Relationships change, who we love changes, even intellectual knowledge that shapes our subjective universe is constantly undergoing change, as we learn new notions or change existing ones with updated information, let's say we always believed there was no life on Mars and then tomorrow one of the Mars Landers takes a photograph of the remains of a fossilised chicken. Our subjective view of the universe changes.

We take it for granted that all living creatures have some semblance of consciousness. Unlike intelligence, we have no real way of measuring consciousness when referring to it in the definition of the 'self-aware version' rather than the medical consciousness that we can record as brain activity.

To exclude the possibility of confusing the two I would like to continue to use the term 'spirit' when referring to the consciousness that makes you who you are, your life, your individuality memories, emotions, and that which drives your decisions and personality.

I honestly do not claim to know if our individual spirit continues after we die, I like to think it does but my ideas on that would fill another book, the question of whether it retains its faculties and its memories, whether it simply dies forever or is even just erased and whether we pass on to another whole new life is moot. But I am thoroughly convinced that I am more than simply a bag of skin with bones and muscles making me move, and I am driven by more complexities than is necessary to survive; to simply, eat and reproduce, and I am sure you are too. The demand for knowledge is an example of a greater complexity. It could be argued that the drive for greater knowledge is an extension of the survival instinct, however being the premium life form on this planet, our risk of destruction as a species by another species is somewhat diminished, as for now we strive to attain knowledge that is purely superficial in as much as it is knowledge that would not aid our survival.

Trying not to stray from the topic too far, if we accept the fact that all things in the known universe existed in some form in the dormant state of the pre-universe singularity, then we must also conclude that everything that makes up our spiritual components must have existed in that singularity too.

The seeming random explosion of particles must have had a fixed position within the singularity as they were singular in number, time itself was a fixed entity, what the void and the universe would come to expand into would have to be equally resistant to the expansion or equally non-resistant, but I cannot guess the makeup of the void, and it would be futile to try.

By the very nature of a singularity, all spirits now segregated by physical individuality must also have existed in that singularity as a combined singular spirit.

None of this so far, although admittedly heavily embroidered with 'wishy-washy new age thought' is in any way straying from what we know in all modern day science. It is entirely theoretical, that is true but is still a scientifically sound principle and not an extreme pro-theism point of view. I hope you will agree and by definition of scientific theory where all theories are considered valid until they are disproved by eminent scientists, this has been the principle standing of theoretical science for hundreds of years.

It is at this point I will throw in something that is abstractly open to dismissal, but equally still plausible. What if that universal spirit was equally self-aware in its previous 'singularity' state?

What if every consciousness that currently exists, will exist and has ever existed, existed within the singularity and was our shared spirit. It would be an entity consisting of the consciousness of the entire universe from every moment in time.

And since the spirit is not bound by physical laws then a developed spirit with fluid consciousness could be contained within a singularity as the only functioning entity.

Would that not be 'God' by most people's definitions?

If not God, then at least in a sense of collective consciousness that separates cognitive life from the inanimate, then surely a form of *Proto-Anthropos* in the purely spiritual sense.

When I refer to God, it is no religious doctrine, nor dogma, it has no definition by religious practices created by man, it does not require worship or prayer, I'm talking about simply a consciousness that is greater than our own, the greater consciousness that was once universal and now split into subjective individualism.

Using the principle that 'God' is not some bearded old man sat at a desk surrounded by lovely white clouds, but a universal consciousness that we share, I would like to see now if what The Bible says about creation and God is compatible with our theory and the scientifically understood creation of the universe using the Big Bang theory. I point out now that I don't necessarily subscribe to the big bang as mentioned in

Exploring The Divine, however this doesn't mean I don't believe it, it means I have yet to be convinced, but it's possible.

The mythology of God has done such a remarkable job of rendering the myth the greater part of the experience than the experience itself could sustain, so that we as a species have become afraid of our own legacy, in other words the stories handed down through generations have been so emphatically enforced as 'the truth' that the very substance of truth for which they stand has been lost.

What good man nor beast is a compulsory faith?

In The Biblical Beginning

Where better to start than 'In the Beginning',

I have chosen the Bible as I believe you, my target audience will be somewhat familiar with it, it is also a text that is essential to understand the origins of Lucifer; Lucifer in aspect a Roman name for an Pre-Abrahamic concept in today's culture. Later I go on to pre-date the Bible with more ancient writings from the Mesopotamian area and the earliest civilisation records that we currently have access to. These records are that of the Sumerians, but to keep my average reader within his comfort zones of experience, I would offer, at this moment comparisons to texts that he should be familiar with, that would be The Bible, or more specifically the Old Testament.

Even if you are not the most avid of Bible readers, even if you have never seen a Bible in your life, the odds are you know the opening lines, 'In the beginning, God created the heavens and the earth, so on and so forth, blah, blah blah…Let there be light'.

Now I doubt you need it explaining to you that the Bible was not written in English, in fact, the amalgamated texts that we currently know as *The Bible* were written in Hebrew, Arabic appended to Roman and Greek Gods, distributed from Greece, translated into English, and edited to suit the purposes of the particular religious order you discovered it in, then even in English it has been translated into a modern text, if you tried to read an English bible from as recently as 1600 I doubt most of us would be able to understand a word of it.

You may not be a scholar of ancient language and neither am I and you may well speak fluently another language to your own, I do not.

However, one thing I do know about language especially protolinguistic is this; it does not translate exactly word for word. Some languages have words that have no translation into English and vice-versa. Some words have multiple meanings when translated.

Many languages have words that have more than one definition, usually there is a subtle difference that can be obtained by the native speaker which 'just' by the context of the conversation would differentiate the speakers intent on such words. I highlighted the word 'just' above as it is one such word, it can mean 'simply' or 'justifiable' or 'pertaining to'.

When we look at simple ancient language, it has not yet evolved its nuances that make translation simple in modern day languages.

For example if we simply choose a common component word such as '*Water*', which when used by someone who may be trying to do their best 'English' from another country could be used to describe any kind of liquid, such as the sea, a river, a drink, fluidity, the ocean, crying or spit.

When someone is trying to speak another language we often use the context surrounding the word to determine what it is they really mean, for example, 'His eyes filled with water' - we would know that the person was referring to tears, rather than the abstract meaning of someone trying to fill an eyeball with water.

Worse when the person who wrote this statement is no longer around to clarify or contextualise what they have said and instead we have to make assumptions based on the logic of context.

The hermetic texts are full of words that have many meanings, in such a sense as I stated with the water analogy above and even the first few lines of what we simply read to be 'In the beginning God created the Heavens, and the Earth' can have many alternative meanings.

The Hebrew Old Testament reads this

> *"bə rê šîṯ bā rā 'ĕ lō hîm; 'êṯ haš šā ma yim wə 'êṯ hā 'ā reṣ. wə hā 'ā reṣ, hā yə ṯāh ṯō hū wā ḇō hū, wə ḥō šeḵ 'al- pə nê ṯə hō wm; wə rū aḥ 'ĕ lō hîm, mə ra ḥe pēṯ 'al- pə nê ham mā yim."*

Whose traditional translation is

> *"At the beginning God created the heavens and the Earth. The earth was untamed and shapeless."*

Seems simple enough?

The book of Genesis I'm sure you know is the Biblical version of the creation of the universe as described by men passing down information from 'God' knows where.

So with that in mind let's try to work out, where this part of the Bible came from, and in my mind it's only possible real origins were that.

A. It was a collection of fabricated stories by man.
B. It was philosophised/theorised by one or many people.
C. It was observed and later documented.
D. It was told to us by God himself.

It is strange to think that out of the four possibilities that **D.** would be so popular.

However, I'm not here to diminish faith I am here to explore it, I am personally theological but in this book I will try to be objective where we are considering the possibility of a greater being.

It is somewhat laughable isn't it, given the three most likely scenarios, man for thousands of years has chosen to believe that which is by evidence least likely.

But don't despair at man's stupidity, it really may be a relatively sound principle and here's why.

The first two are all equally plausible; C. is fairly unlikely for reasons that I will explain in a minute. But as with all translations and interpretations of ancient texts they are subject to the objectives or understanding of those doing the translating along with the translation problems described above. That is to be said of the whole of the Bible or the whole of any other ancient text.

In its Hebrew form, the first three words 'In the beginning' the Hebrew version actually reads 'be-reish-it', it's primary, literal translation is actually in head of', not 'in the beginning,' so it is understood to be equivalent to the English 'a head of', 'ahead of' being a positional time descriptor for 'before'. It seems to have been changed to 'in the beginning' for dramatic effect, that's artistic license don't you know, but was probably contextualised based on the following words 'God created…'.

Again what the next word in Hebrew actually reads is 'bara' which means 'created,' but unlike our English verbs Hebrew and many other languages assign a gender to words, as it happens 'bara' is of a male gender, so it is understood to read 'he created', strangely though it now follows with the word 'Elohim' which is Hebrew for 'god' or is one of the names of God. (For future reference, 'EL (el)' is often the shortened version of things relating to God from the word El-ohim, Ang-el and Micha-el for example), more details of this are in my previous book ***Exploring the Divine.***

So our literal translation thus far, it reads 'in head of creation, God…'. Which is fairly uncomfortable word usage to the native English speaker, so it is assumed that it is much like

French to English translation, where sometimes the order in which we say words is reversed.

In English, we would say "red wine" however the French would say "vin rouge" (wine red) with the more definitive descriptor first.

So to be made more 'English' friendly 'in head of creation God' becomes 'at first, God created…' or as it is more commonly known 'In the beginning God created…'

Following that dramatic start Genesis continues 'the heavens and the earth' or as written in Hebrew:-

"et hashamayim ve'et ha'aretz wə hā 'ā reṣ,"

Which figuratively means 'everything' but specifically reads 'heavens and the earth'.

We even use the figure of speech 'the heavens and the earth' nowadays in English it is a common turn of phrase which is intended to mean 'everything' or 'anything', but what makes this a strange turn of phrase in the original Hebrew is it actually says the *"heaven and the earth"*.

Now even in our modern day understanding of the term 'the heavens' we can equally consider that definition as being 'space' in both the extra-terrestrial sense and all ethereal gaps between matter (air or the aether etc.), therefore it is one of those words that has many meanings including, air, Heaven, the sky or above. And for that matter 'earth' may also not be refering to only our planet but all physical matter, such as land, rocks, the ground, other planets and stars, we even call 'dirt' earth in English. And so the statement could well be all encompassing 'heavens and earth', rather than specifically being the sky and the land or the planet on which we live, could mean space and matter.

So how accurate is that ancient story of creation contained in the dismissed scientifically *Old Testament* now we have revised it using our more modern concepts of creation, something we as a species were not in a better position to do until recently? And what of the spiritual consciousness contained within a singularity, is that measurable or considered in these early lines of the bible? With punctuation 'In the head of creation God, The heavens and the earth'.

You see how I have changed 'ahead' into the translation of 'in the head', as this is yet another translation of 'be-reish-it' a translation that I purposely kept away from you until this all comes together. Our most famous opening lines of a book in the world could equally be read 'In the mind of God was the universe.' This is certainly metaphysical concepts that we philosophise even to this day with new supported ideas of *quantum theory*.

Isn't that familiar with what I said when describing the singularity? All things combined into a single entity, spirit, matter and space metaphysically? If true, then we are left with three of our possibilities, as the premise that it was all simply made up by ancient storytellers is a little too close to modern ideas to be randomly invented, maybe it was a lucky guess, Im not at a point to conclude absolutely, nor do I assume, will I ever be.

So now we are left with either it was philosophised, it was observed, or it told to us by God himself, as it does not seem likely that a pure guess or story could be so close to the evidence we have today. Its not impossible, but it is unlikely.

So let us see if we can rule out another one of the more reasonable logical possibilities, like the famous Sherlock Holmes quote penned by Sir Arthur Conan Doyle "Once you eliminate the impossible, whatever remains, no matter how improbable, must be the truth".

Ruling out the next one can be quite simple, and so I can close this without any elaborate build up and hidden meaning.

If it was observed then the only entity that could have possibly observed it, would be the collective spirit contained within the singularity itself as nothing else existed in the void outside of the entity. So C. and D. are effectively the same things, the observer could only be God Himself as in the previous chapter I explained that a single conscious entity within the singularity would be considered God by all definitions, so by that concept I will combine C into D.

Bizarrely, we are now only left with B and D.

B. It was philosophised by one or many people.

D. It was told to us by God himself.

Going back to B. We can at any point philosophise, so that will always remain plausible, but by the very nature of philosophy, it is equally plausible that the only reason we can 'philosophise' this quandary is simply because we experienced it under our collective consciousness while within the singularity where all things existed as one, and rather than new thought, it is actually an inherited memory coming to life, triggered by our debates on the topic, because we concluded that all things thought or 'ever to be thought' also already existed in this singularity. Our very being is at this point a part of God's consciousness separated into individual consciousness brought about by the big bang. This inherent knowledge was while we were collectively God in our singularity.

Using this premise, Mr Holmes would make his conclusion that logically the only remaining truth is 'It was told to us by God himself.' And the statement is the word of God.

Now that I have proposed this possibility and explained the rationale behind it, for fun let's carry on and see what else the ancients had to say about Creation of the universe and see if it ties in with anything else we have now come to discover.

Genesis continues:-

"wə hā 'ā reṣ, hā yə ṯāh ṯō hū wā ḇō hū, wə ḥō šeḵ 'al-pə nê ṯə hō wm; wə rū aḥ 'ĕ lō hîm, mə ra ḥe pēṯ 'al-pə nê ham mā yim."

Which is confusingly translated to 'Now the earth was formless and empty. Darkness was on the surface of the deep. God's spirit was hovering over the surface of the waters'.

The Earth, in this case, described as 'boho' meaning anything that is formless and empty, even if we take the concept that the earth as a planet was formless and empty, it doesn't really fit well with the description of a solid object does it, it does, however, work very well when describing matter not yet in its physical state as we imagine it, but as a component of the singularity philosophical, in this imaginary state matter was yet to take form.

Darkness or obscurity was on the surface of the deep, I believe is an elaborate description of the void that would have surrounded the singularity which even today is an inconceivable notion other than as a 'darkness' or 'choshek' the word choshek which as well as meaning 'darkness' also means 'obscurity'. This obscurity is on the surface of the surrounding areas, furthermore the deep is not describing the seas as we would interpret it, because as the word 'Tehom' in its original written form can also mean abyss, and could also describe either the unlimited depth of the content of the singularity, or the unlimited distance of the surrounding void.

You can see only a few words into the first couple of lines of the Bible, with slight adjustment and equally valid translation from its source in Hebrew, just how many words can have completely different interpretations and how we automatically translate them based upon the context of one keyword, which is then used to formulate the next. In the context of creating a world, we would use land and seas, but if interpreted in the context of the creation of the universe, then this works equally well at redefining the biblical texts from outdated nonsense into the current scientific model.

So which stance would you now take? We know that the standard interpretation of the creation of the earth according to our present version of Genesis is wrong by all scientific accounts, the earth is universally not such a great shake in terms of creation; not like it once was when it was the centre of the universe, and God's premium pet project. Earth is just one of many billion 'Goldilocks-zone' planets likely to contain life. You could argue that my claims are equally wrong, but then why has such a text been held sacred for such a long time, stories have come and gone, Gods from all regions have been classified as mythology, yet the battle to defend this particular God as being valid continues today, even though, the likes of Thor, Zeus and Odin have fallen by the wayside.

Supporting this theory that Genesis is possibly an ancient account of real events would not automatically diminish any atheist viewpoints you may have if that's your chosen path, remember the book is not what you object to, it's what the book represents, so if we can work together to prove that the book has been misinterpreted then that if anything lends weight to your argument. However, we still will have the marvellous mystery of who wrote the damn thing to solve. We shall continue with the translation and see where that takes us.

What is interesting next is that the text specifically states 'God's Spirit', not God as a physical entity, but as a spirit. The spirit of God was moving 'rachaph' which also means rested or relaxed, what if this is describing not God at work, but returning to a state of rest?

The Bible has clearly chosen one particular context that suits one perspective when translated into English, but look at this chart below and you can see multiple ways to change the Entire context, leading me to my versions below.

wə·hā·'ā·reṣ	The Earth	Land	Matter	Soil	Substance
hā·yə·ṯāh	Fall Out	Come to pass	Became	Came out	Will be
ṯō·hū	Formless	Without Shape			
wā·ḇō·hū	Void	Empty			
wə·ḥō·šeḵ	And Darkness	Obscure	Hidden		
al-	Over	Upon	Above		
pə·nê	The Surface	face	facia		
ṯə·hō·wm	Of the deep	Sea	Abyss		
wə·rū·aḥ	And the Spirit	Breath	Wind	Air	
'ĕ·lō·hîm	Of God				
mə·ra·ḥe·p̄eṯ	Grew Soft	Relaxed	Rested	Moved upon	Went to
al-	Over	Upon	Above		
pə·nê	The Surface	face	facia		
ham·mā·yim.	The Waters	Sea	Liquid		

In the context of a scientific creation of the universe from a singularity, it is equally able to be translated thus.

> *"Land came out of the formless void upon the surface of the abyss, and the breath of god grew soft upon the the surface of the water".*

Please now imagine throwing a stone into a pool of still water in relation to '*The Big Bang*', the initial explosion of movement in the water, the expanding circles of wave, followed by the resting of the water.

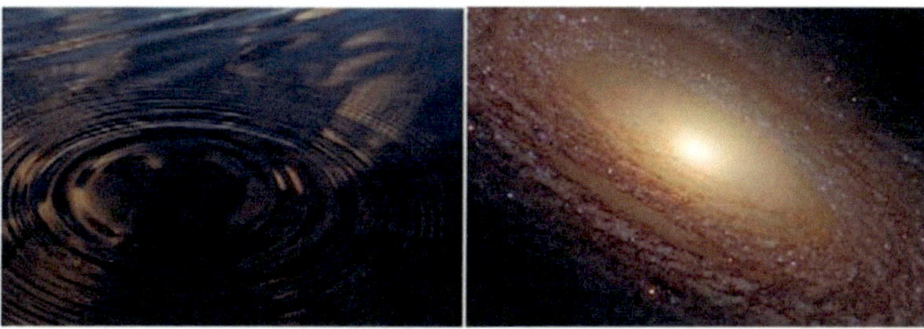

That is exactly how *The Big Bang* would have occurred but described obviously on a much more comprehensible scale, and put into a context that is less scientifically spoken as we would describe it today, you can clearly see the description of matter created from nothing in a 'the breath of God' outward motion which began to rest much like a stone thrown into the waters, the entropy of gods power reaching a rested state.

Let there be light

way·yō·mer 'ĕ·lō·hîm yə·hî 'ō·wr; way·hî- 'ō·wr. way·yar 'ĕ·lō·hîm 'eṯ- hā·'ō·wr kî- ṭō·wḇ; way·yaḇ·dêl 'ĕ·lō·hîm, bên hā·'ō·wr ū·ḇên ha·ḥō·šeḵ. way·yiq·rā 'ĕ·lō·hîm lā·'ō·wr yō·wm, wə·la·ḥō·šeḵ qā·rā lā·yə·lāh; way·hî- 'e·reḇ way·hî- ḇō·qer yō·wm 'e·ḥāḏ. p̄

Spoken by God, there shall be light, and there was light, to see Gods light was good, and different, and God divided God from the darkness and shouted day, light and night, and there was the first day.

We have established that the breath of god is used as an analogy for the explosive power of creation, so things carried upon that breath would be described as the words of god.

Therefore, anything proclaimed as spoken by God, are descriptions of things that were created out of that event

"God's words were light, and so light was seen and this was good, it created a division to the darkness and obscurity that was before and was called day and night.

Hebrew	Meaning	or	or	or
way·yō·mer	Was Said	Proclaim	Speak	say
'ĕ·lō·hîm	God	God's		
yə·hî	Let There be	become	be	
'ō·wr	Light			
way·hî-	Was become	became	came to pass	was
'ō·wr	Light			
way·yar	Was Seen	to see		
'ĕ·lō·hîm	God	God's		
'eṯ- hā·'ō·wr	Light			
kî-	that	for	when	
ṭō·wḇ;	Good	Pleasant	Agreeable	
way·yaḇ·dêl	Was Divided	Separated		
'ĕ·lō·hîm	God			
bên	From	Interval	Separator	interval
hā·'ō·wr	Light			
ū·ḇên	had been	from	Interval	
ha·ḥō·šeḵ	The Darkness	Obscurity	Hidden	
way·yiq·rā	Was Called	Call	Proclaim	Named
'ĕ·lō·hîm	God			
lā·'ō·wr	The Light	Light		
yō·wm	Day			
wə·la·ḥō·šeḵ	The Darkness	Obscurity	Hidden	
qā·rā	Was Called	Call	Proclaim	Named
lā·yə·lāh	Night			
way·hî-	Was become	became	came to pass	was
'e·reḇ	Evening			
way·hî	Was become	became	came to pass	was
ḇō·qer	Morning			
yō·wm	Day			
'e·ḥāḏ.	One			

Gustave Doré's illustration for Milton's Paradise Lost, V, 1006-1015: Satan yielding before Gabriel

Lucifer's Mythology

When we consider Lucifer's current incarnation it is an amalgamation of the mysticism of many civilisations and cultures dating back to prehistory.

It is a mishmash their legends and often a bizarre conjecture of more modern outright delusion. The Neo-Luciferian movement has less to do with these mythological personifications than Holywood would have you believe. Instead, it is to many a choice of personal development akin to other higher spirit studies such as Kabbalism, Buddhism and even a none dogmatic version of Christianity. It is a rapidly growing phenomena here in the new millennia as people reject conventional historical dogma and embrace man's ineffable rights to his personally derived moral sensibility.

Lucifer is both literally and metaphorically is *"the herald of the new dawn"*.

As we sit on this cusp of the age of Aquarius, I believe the rise in luciferianism is a fulfilment of a long foretold and cyclic prophecy, written in nearly all hermetic texts, written in the stars above and the reflection of the microcosm in the macrocosm, as above such is below.

Modern Luciferianism is diverse; it can simply be for those who wish to remain separate from the mystical and occult practices, a study in self-fulfilment. For others, it is a philosophy and an engaging practice of unrestricted mystical and magical exploration. It is neither good nor evil, in fact, it is the very thing that breaks away from this duality. It is the recognition that duality is simply a divided expression of the whole. Too long have we allowed division to separate us from our fellow man by looking and exalting that which we are and vilifying that which we are not. If this unification of mankind or even life as a whole under one sky is evil to you, then it is my opinion that you have not evolved.

In their literature, the Gnostics of the first to the fourth century, presented Lucifer as quite a righteous character, unfairly maligned by the establishing and politically organising Abrahamic faiths.

The personality and character traits that represent Lucifer today were primarily developed in the poem ***Paradise Lost*** by John Milton published in 1667 as an epic verse comprising of ten books. Earlier literature that expanded lucifers conception as demonic was yet another poem, this time from the 14th century writer Dante Alighieri, ***Dante's Inferno***, telling of Dante's voyage through the nine circles of Hell, guided by the long since dead Roman poet Virgil.

Lucifer in this story is not portrayed in the way we understand from the claimed 'less fictional' Biblical legend. No! In ***Inferno*** he is the first conception of sin and therefore, the embodiment of all that is sin for all time then to pass. The most evil creator of sin and therefore the father of all following wrongdoing. Sin that is within us was derived from the source within Lucifer. In ***Inferno*** he is portrayed as a giant titanic winged demon trapped in a lake of ice that engulfs his feet, he flaps his wings in an eternal cry for freedom only to create the draught that keeps the ice frozen.

For the purposes of the title of the book ***Exegesis of Lucifer,*** readers will expect the mythology of the person or deity to be explained or at least covered somewhat and this is what I intend to do with this chapter.

I will try to cover as many of the stories that are the fuel of the endless debates in luciferian circles, and as best I possibly can, without expressing a preference. Preference after all is your choice to make, it is as valid as all the rest.

The name Lucifer was given to this idol by the Romans, I use the word idol in both senses of meaning, Lucifer is his Latin name and most popular. In almost all cases the translation of the name in some way refers to *'Morning Star'*, *'Light bringer'*, *'Son of the morning'* or *'Light Bearer'* and this is strongly, if not undoubtedly believed to be a direct reference to the planet Venus.

Gods in those days were either the greater celestial bodies, stars, planets or celestial events such as eclipses; or they were children of elements such as Air, Earth, Water, Fire and Light which were the primordial Gods, Titans if you like being as they were formed as a result of our ancestral philosophers conceiving the universal substance and then deliberating upon a later order of creation.

Creation usually began with some form of void or absence of physicality, this ultimately will be the highest of the ordinal gods, its supremacy will either be passive or active in the later creation by the application of will, the primordial will.

After a will has been established it would then continue with the creation of the primary elementals that would be the 'children of the void' conceptually. In mythology child elements develop stories in the same way children of men would develop them, these would enable the continuation of legend through word of mouth prior to the development of writing, embellishment would allow both ease of tuition and secrecy of the actual meaning of the parables depending on the intent of the tutor.

Whether or not these legends were truly intended as a fable, or if it was just our stupidity somewhere in time that lead us to believe them as actual events involving real characters will never be known. That said, when you look at the science hidden within these parables, metaphors or stories, you cannot help but to come to the conclusion that our ancestral philosophers and scientists were definitely more advanced in concepts of creation, the universe, physics and astrology than we give them credit for, and so the blame for this grievous loss in translation has to be attributed to our more recent ancestors than the authors themselves who do seem to get a hard time, suggesting that they were talking nonsense. It is true they were, but they knew they were and it is the interpreters who have now lost the plot.

After the creation of the elements which were the building blocks of substance, it was through astrological observations that ancient scientists applied their interpretation of the program being shown on this ancient version of a TV set which we call 'the heavens' that these scripts began to be written. The great thinkers of the time would consider the regulatory nature of the night sky, fixed and distant objects such as the stars within our galaxy and the galaxies beyond which to their naked eye would in most cases appear as stars. This ordinal precision was interpreted as being a part of the story of the universe. Larger objects obviously received more significance, our sun being holiest of all, must therefore be either a god, the God, or a messenger from other gods such as its parent gods, the void, Titans and so on.

Once established reccurring patterns became known and predictable such as the cyclic nature of the seasons. This gave man the first ability to predict a future based on these celestial observations. Information like this proved invaluable in mans development of civilisation, knowledge for one's tribe such as when to plant seed, when to stockpile food or water for drought, would ensure the success of 'chosen tribes' lead by shamans, wizards, kings who were masters of the unseen arts, so it was beneficial to the soothsayer to keep this knowledge very tight to his chest. The opportunistic and revered man concluded that other gods may give clues to other events, so they mapped and studied the smaller distant objects such as the tiny dots that we call stars.

Certain objects made their presence known by not conforming to the static and predictable nature of the rest of the observed sky, they moved seemingly independently and did not follow the normal annual patterns. These would be the planets contained in our solar system, which we now know work differently because they orbit our sun.

It is clear that the predictions of certain objects means that the scholars in the past studied them long enough to be able to predict events and indeed even know of events that we have only calculated with their help, technology and mathematics. They as best we can guess must have observed and recorded them over several millennia; things such as our galactic rotation, which occurs only every two hundred and fifty million years, according to our estimates something the earth has only completed the cycle of twenty times since its creation yet indeed the astrologers in the past knew far more about the sky than history can give them credit for and I can offer no explanation of how.

Moving objects when compared to the background and static sky passed legend into the characters that formed the constellations. Each constellation was given different names in different cultures, examples would be such as Orion, Scorpio, and many more. Often the physical representation of the creature, item or man would denote its significance at that time of year to the people of the area, Libra would be a time of imbalance or judgement while Aquarius the water bearer could signify floods or heavy rains.

A study that is still observed today in the form of astrology. If you think astrology is a bunch of mumbo jumbo as I admit, I long believed, I certainly now recognise that while the newspapers giving us our daily horoscopes may be rubbish, there is definitely some foundation in the humors of the universe affecting us at least in nature.

So when we hear mythos about the exploits of these heroes of Greece or the Nordic gods, even the Christian Bible, they are primarily the descriptions of celestial events put into metaphors or parables, but this does not mean they are nonsense.

> *The morning star heralds the dawn of the new sun of God; Venus rises slightly before The Sun in the east.*

You may be aware that Egyptians believed their Pharos to be mortal incarnations of the gods, and so they were gods, they were given gods names, and despite their short mortal lives on the planet they would also be attributed with the miraculous astrological legends that preceded their earthly form. By all intents and purposes, anything that happened to that celestial God over thousands of years would be attributed to the mortal man during his lifetime.

The same is true of Jesus or Yeshua, who was indeed a mortal man, of this I have no doubt, most likely a king in the line of the Jewish King David. He may well have had a mortal incarnation many times, but each time he would be considered the current incarnation, in the case of the God Jesus, as we call him, then the most recent incarnation is suggested to be two thousand or so years ago.

This practice is continued today similarly in the case of the Dahlia Llama, who is believed to be the reincarnation of previous Dahlia Llamas.

Jesus, the man, was attributed with the historical attributes of Horus the god and many others, including Lucifer "I am the light of the earth".

Guido Reni's Archangel Michael 1636c

Roman

In Roman mythology, Lucifer is not associated with any devil, in classical depiction he is clearly one of the angels, beautiful, muscular with flowing hair, white swan-like wings, he is the modern day version of an angel.

Sadly *Lucifer101* is repeated almost everywhere, even in this book, so it frustrates me to have to include it, which I do on grounds of being comprehensive, as in the Roman/Latin literal definitions of 'lucem ferre,' where Lucifer has adopted his most common name (Lucifer) and this is also where he gets the synonym *'Light-Bearer'* or *'Light Bringer'* in Latin Lucem or Lux, which means 'light,' and Ferre meaning 'to bear, carry, suffer or endure'.

Combined we get the dative *'Luci'* and the present singular *'Fer'*.

It is difficult to find specific attributes to Lucifer the god in the Roman version beyond this. One of the issues being that in almost all other cultures the light bearer or 'morning star' is unquestionably a pseudonym for the planet Venus. Venus, however, is already a Roman god. Therefore, if the planet Venus is also Lucifer in Latin, there is no context to establish his legend under Roman history. Furthermore Venus to the Romans is female, a goddess, it would make no sense that the Romans would give Venus the epithet of Lucifer if they saw the single planet as two distinct entities, although there is as always strong evidence of many names being used for the same celestial entity at different times of the day and it remains a deliberation that certainly should have been resolved by the times of the Roman Empire that the morning star and evening star were one in the same celestial body.

It is suggested that the name Lucifer predates the name Venus in Roman culture; almost nothing documents a transition between the two. The morning star has a counterpart the evening star and in the works of Pliny the Elder wrote in 23-79 CE 'The star called Venus, when it rises in the morning is given the name Lucifer, but when it shines at sunset it is called Vesper'.

Logically you could not call Venus the morning star in the evening, although it would be unusual for these entities to change gender. There would usually be a legend of one killing, defeating or in some way banishing the other.

Even in Christian culture Lucifer became Satan only after his fall from heaven, a duality. So it would seem that the mere adoption of the literal translation from the morning star (Venus) is sufficient for him to be aligned with the better-documented history from other cultures.

Lucifer is according to Abrahamic lore an angel who fell from heaven and by the direct translation of the Hebrew Ang-El which means *"messenger of God"* Lucifer would herald the coming of a god in the morning and as I believe, depending on the astrological location it would be the word of God foretelling many events because the shapes of celestial bodies would indicate to the astrologers of ancient times, the written heavenly alphabet of God, and the stars arrangements create the word.

LVNA LVCIF (Moon Light)

Segue slightly at this point to mention the goddess LVNA LVCIF (Moon Light) who appears on a Roman coin as depicted below.

The coin depicting the Luna is the goddess of The Moon and yet also Diana, and Juno are epithets of The Moon, so there is actually a president of a single celestial entity having more than one title in Roman theology. The coin dates to AD 253 to AD260. Even the Greeks reinforce this with The Moon who is both Selene and Artemis in their mythologies.

Diana is associated with Lucifer as a consort, brother and possibly a son, this kind of illogical association is commonplace in ancient texts simply because of the cyclic nature of celestial observation. A father will become a son, The Sun will rise in a morning as a child, in the evening it will descend into 'the other place, Hell, the underworld' due to the

Earth's rotation and the possible lack of awareness or maybe it is simply a conceptual opposition that man speculates what is under the earth from where the observer stands.

'Underground' or the underworld is the place where the dead go; logically observing celestial bodies movement across the sky due to the Earth's rotation is a three-stage event, ascension, glory and descension or demise which was associated with death and rebirth at a later point.

The very three words used in astrology are repeated as descriptions of biblical characters.

Ascension: (to ascend), rise up towards heavens. Oppose descension.

Exaltation: the sign of the zodiac in which the most positive influence of a planet is expressed.

Descension: Astrology - the part of the zodiac in which the influence of a planet is weakest.

In the 1899 book Aradia, Gospel of the Witches, by Charles Godfrey Leland, Leland a notable folklore and occult writing describes this relationship as follows.

> *Diana was the first created before all creation; in her were all things; out of herself, the first darkness, she divided herself; into darkness and light she was divided. Lucifer, her brother and son, herself and her other half, was the light.*

> *And when Diana saw that the light was so beautiful, the light that was her other half, her brother Lucifer, she yearned for it with exceeding great desire. Wishing to receive the light again into her darkness, to swallow it up in rapture, in delight, she trembled with desire. This desire was the Dawn.*
>
> *But Lucifer, the light, fled from her, and would not yield to her wishes; he was the light which files into the most distant parts of heaven, the mouse which flies before the cat.*
>
> *Then Diana went to the fathers of the Beginning, to the mothers, the spirits who were before the first spirit, and lamented unto them that she could not prevail with Lucifer. And they praised her for her courage, they told her that to rise she must fall; to become the chief of goddesses she must become a mortal.*
>
> *And in the ages, in the course of time, when the world was made, Diana went on earth, as did Lucifer.*

A conclusion I have drawn to fill in the gaps of the Lineage of the Roman version of Lucifer would be to associate the Greek gods with their Roman counterpart to see if there is any fit due to the lack of historical evidence found of their mindset regarding Lucifer. The Roman god of the dawn was *Aurora* the reasoning behind this will be explained in the following section of Greek Mythos, and rather than stray off into Greek too early I shall simply tell you some of Aurora's attributes.

Her brother was the Sol (Sun) And her Sister was Luna (Moon). The word Aurora to us is mostly associated with the northern lights whose effect is caused by the interaction of charged particles from The Sun with atoms in the upper atmosphere. In the north and southern regions, it is respectively called *Aurora Borealis* or Northern Lights and Aurora Australis or Southern Lights. To those that rarely got to see this phenomenon, it would be the light from the horizon heralding the dawn or the evening sunset thus establishing the parents of Lucifer as being a mother Dawn and a father Sun-set.

Her name is derived from the Latin word 'Ausus' which means simply dawn. Interestingly she was considered the mother of the four winds, which you will read more of in Lucifer's Greek counterpart Phosphorus. More interestingly she later got absorbed into an earlier goddess *Mater Matuta* goddess of spring, birth, the sea and the morning.

Evidence of Mater Matuta dates back to four thousand years before the birth of Christ and into the stone age, yet she is depicted in reliefs and statues from that period in a very recognisable mother and child pose.

Mater, literally meaning mother and Matuta which means morning. If we look deeper into name meanings in this case we find that 'mata' means 'gift of God' that has alternative Hebrew variants? such as 'Matai' which similarly but directly means 'Gift of Yahweh'. The names Mataleen and Mataleena are synonymous with the phrase 'Of Magdalene'. Mother, Gift of God, Of Magdalene. Magdalene often in modern times thought to be associated or directly interpreted as meaning 'prostitute' and is *kind of* offensive, but that is a very patriarchal interpretation of the translation 'Fallen woman'. We should consider the fallen woman in the same context as we perceive Lucifer as a fallen angel.

We get words such as matrimony, marital, marriage, maternity from this name, some of which we would also call 'to marry'. Mary would be the archetype spouse and natural mother of all spiritual and celestial bodies. Always remember that all these fables have a beginning, middle and end beginning with a child or infant, innocence or a Virgin, a rise to power, becoming a father or mother then a demise or fall and then a rebirth or renewal. Gender aside these are the attributes of all legends related to Lucifer, Jesus, Horus and many others. In Christianity, which I firmly believe is based on these legends, Jesus's life begins with Mary the virgin and ends with Mary Magdalene, the fallen woman. The cycle completes in the constellation of Virgo on an annual scale or in the case of the goddess of the morning star, giving birth to The Sun god by Venus rising before The Sun in the morning and heralding its demise in the evening, Venus the mother.

We'll come back to that later.

Greek

Phosphorus

The Greeks certainly had more to say about Phosphorus than we know the Romans did. Again the literal translation is light(phos) bringer(phoros), this provides sufficient association to be classed as a Lucifer class character and in Greek mythology is directly linked to the planet Venus and he has an alternate name of Heosphoros, Heo in this instance meaning 'Dawn'. Venus's orbit lies between The Sun and the Earth and is always low in the sky in both the morning and at dusk when it appears to follow The Sun rather than heralding it. And so becomes the Evening star as Venus is from Earth's perspective the brightest celestial object other than The Sun and The Moon. Phosphorus' legend and lineage get a little confusing as if it's not already. If we take the works of Greek poet Hesiod (750-640 BC), Phosphorus was the son of Astraeus and Eos. Astraeus Was a Titan; Titans are primal elements rather than celestial manifestations, he is associated with the four winds and is God of the dusk. As a personal expansion on this I would, class him as the omnipotence of evening and the night, the four winds are to be considered here dimensional domains rather than specifically wind as we know it, much like the wind it is able to imbue itself anywhere, it is a very ethereal concept.

The winds were often to increase their potency towards the evening and so he is imparted with the name "The keeper of the four winds" so he was not the wind itself but wielded it like Zeus wielded lightning bolts. He would be the night sky and is where we get the word astro-logy from, this gives him his distinct association with Venus in its position as the evening star, when Astraeus was as significant to the ancients as a particular time of day.

Eos Sophorous's mother also a Titan was again a more ambient manifestation unlike the physical planets and stars, she was simply the dawn, a Logical mother for the Morningstar and consort for the evening dusk. Her Brother was Helios (The Sun) and her sister Selene (The Moon) and here we establish the very distinct elements that make up our Sky, The Sun, Moon, and Night all complete our family tree for the child Sophoros.

Prometheus

In Greek mythos, Lucifer is aligned with the character Prometheus. In their version of creationism, there was *in the beginning* only 'Chaos' which is equivalent to the biblical void. It was without form and insubstantial and the origin of all things, shapeless and without order.

Prometheus Bound Jacob Jordaens 1640

The similarities of events unfolding cannot be denied, whether this then lends further credence to the descriptions written in ancient texts being an actual event or simply a well-travelled legend cannot be taken for granted.

Modern Greeks tend to take their mythos without the literal impetus of other cultures although in a later chapter I do suggest that one of their believed 'real' most famous sons may

actualy be myth, and they do not get offended when you refer to their former gods as mere legend as other cultures seem to.

Greece and its islands lie just a few hundred navigable miles across the Mediterranean Sea and are in close proximity to the Middle East, Iran, Iraq, Egypt, Syria and the origins of the Judeo-Christian creation systems, in particular Babylon where the King Nebuchadnezzar II, created the largest and most multicultural city in the world at that time.

Nebuchadnezzar actively sought the great thinkers and philosophers from all the surrounding empires to exchange in discourse and share scientific, theological and philosophical concepts, this lead to one of the truly great industrious times of human civilisation. Greek trade routes by sea or via Turkey were well established at the time which provided an excellent opportunity for two major and advanced philosophical cultures to exchange the best that classic culture had to offer.

The symbol we used today to represent chaos is indicative of 'a void from which all things are created' you can see it easily representing the *'Big Bang'* even.

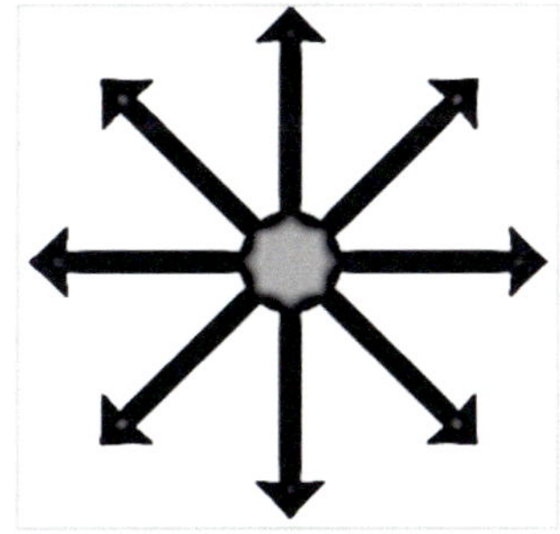

Amongst its name it is known as *Arms of Chaos*, the *Arrows of Chaos*, the *Chaos Star, the Chaos Cross*, or the *Symbol of Eight*.

However this symbol when used to represent specifically our modern day concept of chaos in symbolism, only came into play in the

1970's in a fantasy novel written by Michael Moorcock and its eight points are I think purely coincidentally reminiscent of the Star of Venus which has links back to 2000BCE, equally and obviously the symbol has been associated with many things such as compass directions for a very long time.

It is worth mentioning that the word Chaos can be broken down into Cha and Os as explained in ETD Cha or Chi is related to Life energy and flow, in Greek Chi is the 22nd letter of their alphabet (pronounced Kai or key), giving us a segue into the Egyptian Key of life or Ankh and is a Greek reference in astronomy to the 22nd star in a constellation. Os signifies a male gender in Greek.

Out of Chaos came Erebus, Erebus is associated with darkness and shadows, by default we tend to imagine the void as black, whereas the Greek theologists realised the duality between night and day would not allow something as descriptive as darkness to exist prior to creation without its equal of light. Ereb-Us; Us would, like 'OS' denote the masculine, but is generally associated with Latin suffixes and Ereb in Hebrew denotes a Friday evening. It is the evening before the Sabbath. It also translates to Eve, as in the night before 'Christmas Eve'and here we also have Eve of Adam and Eve fame, one of Gods first children and of course, we consider Eve to be female.

Erebus is married (for want of a better term) to Nyx, the primordial goddess of the night, and Erebus's own sister. To be fair there wasn't really a lot of choices back then, and while we attach human relationships to these principles, it is after all a metaphorical story. And so night and darkness are joined together in an eternal association, between them they gave birth to other associated concepts Hypnos(Sleep) and Thanatos(death), Nyx is easily associated with the Egyptian god Nut who seemingly forms the canopy in which stars are created, she is also associated with the milky way, the divine Mother. The Milky Way, our galaxy gets its name because for those lucky enough to get a very clear starry night the band that forms the horizontal axis of our galaxy can be seen as a massive band of stars spanning the centre of the sky. The Romans and Greeks associated this with the lactation of life's milk, from a god's bosom, such as Nyx and Nut, This blessing or state of happiness made us 'El-late-ed' (blessed with the milk of gods kindness). The Romans called it *"Via Lactea"* (Way of Milk), the Greeks are accredited with even the word Galaxy (see Lax as in Lactate) which they called *"Kyklos"* meaning milky circle.

If Lax is the milk of the night sky which we know is created by the distant stars, you can see the word association to the Latin *"Lux"* of light.

Erebus had three siblings Gaia (the earth) Tartarus (the abyss) and Eros (desire). However, the lineage we are interested in follows down to Gaia.

Gaia is Mother Earth, matter. The word Mother is a derivative of the word 'matter' in French and Latin *"Mátre"* you can see the connection here in form.

Gaia is known for her motherly nature, the lactation of the Milky Way is associated with her amply depicted breasts in artworks, her heavily pregnant tummy often depicting her as cradling the earth within as though it is her unborn child. She is the giver of life and those that give life are *"Martyrs"*.

However this should not be taken that Gaia being mother earth is a reference to our planet alone, but to all matter in the universe and so shows that the Ancient Greeks in their version of the story of creation were aware even way back then that the light they saw from the stars and Galaxies unfathomable distances away, were more substantial than the ethereal context of pure light itself. They knew that the stars and planets were formed from physical objects of matter and that is a wonder in itself.

Referencing back to the Chapter *"the eternal torment of being god"* we discussed the symbols for the four prime elements Fire, Air, Earth and water. The very feminine symbol for earth is defined by a gender. It is the very vaginal shaped downward pointing "V" and more artistic symbols of this tend to incorporate particularly motherly aspects such as things pertaining to the womb or reproduction. Gaia is often associated with trees, the tree of life and so her personal symbols and iconographs will usually incorporate a tree or a very evidently mother in waiting with blossoming with unborn or newly born child such as the Mary Mother of god Character is associated with both Gia, Mother Earth and Virgo as a constellation.

Mother earth, Gaia had children with Uranus. Uranus at the time was not the planet we know today, but the sky or heavens. Father Sky, therefore, is in opposition with Mother Earth, the beginning of his name Ur(uran) and is synonymous with Air and gives us such words as Uranography which is a branch of astrology specifically related to mapping the positions of the stars and galaxies as a science. Ur was also a city or major 'Ur-ban' centre of Sumerian culture located in modern day Iraq(Ur-aq) founded in approximately 6000 to 3800BCE (man's Bronze age). Ur is more famously known as the area of Mesopotamia that advanced modern civilisation, it was the birthplace of these astrological studies that later evolved into the Abrahamic religions of Christianity, Judaism and Islam as it is reputed to be specifically the city of Ur Kasdim which in the book of genesis is the birthplace of Abraham (Ibrahim) and was occupied by people known as the Chaldees.

Lucifer before the Lord, by Mihály Zichy

Plato

Plato, we are lead to believe was a Greek philosopher and mathematician who is known as the father of western philosophy. We get the word philosopher from Philo-Sophia. Philo means liking for and Sophia means wisdom.

It may be contrary to all current opinion, but I believe that Plato never existed or if he did, he existed in the same way Jesus did, a man attributed with the legend of the gods. It is strange that we take some ancient history as fact and others as mythos. Plato I believe was a god, most likely a disambiguation of Pluto, Roman god of the underworld in classical mythology also known as Hades.

This underworld connection is enough for me to associate him with the fallen side of Lucifer. We have an underworld character associated with wisdom, weak I agree, but let me continue. Academics will claim evidence of the man as being a pupil of Socrates and a teacher of Aristotle and I am sure these were people too, but only in the same way we have the holy trinity or the Jesus, Mary and Joseph characters. It is no stretch of the imagination that these three immortal Philosophical gods should be so directly related to each other in timeline and geography.

No, I believe that Plato was the personification of collected wisdom. Plato according to legend was the son of Ariston and Plato was originally named Aristocles, which is very similar to Aristotle, already we begin to get the holy trinity link father/teacher vs. son/student relationship. Plato was descended from a lineage of ancient kings of Athens, namely the line of Codrus, who is considered semi-mythical already, just like the lineage of Jesus whose parents both descended via different routes from ancient kings in the line of David.

Pluto's mother was called Perictione who was a descendant of Solon the lawgiver sounds a bit like Solomon) who was also descended from the line of Codrus.

Perictione is credited with writing herself on the harmony of women in wisdom. Legend has it that Ariston, Plato's father raped Perictione when she was a blossoming virgin, but failed to win her as a wife and so he stopped raping her, 'Apollo appeared to him in a dream, whereupon he left her unmolested until her child was born.'

Does that not sound somewhat familiar? Plato is the son of a fallen virgin, whose birth was prophesied by a messenger of the gods.

Ariston died when Plato was young, similar to the story of Joseph, Jesus's father who disappears from the bible before Jesus begins his ministry.

In his Seventh Letter, Plato notes that his coming of age coincided with the taking of power by the Thirty, remarking, "But a youth under the age of twenty made himself a laughingstock if he attempted to enter the political arena." In Jesus legend 'When he was twelve, Jesus was stirred by the drama of the Passover and was drawn to the temple. Here rabbis would meet to discuss theology, with a likely emphasis on the coming of Messiah. Jesus engaged the older rabbis in a question and answer format, displaying a deep spiritual knowledge that amazed everyone who heard him.'

Similar stories of the age of becoming a man and entering an arena of peers but with dualistic results.

It is not known where or why Plato took his more familiar name; it is suggested that it is taken from the Greek word *platon* which means broad or far reaching and is ascribed to his broad knowledge. More likely it is representative of a collective knowledge as I suggest, the broad or far-reaching knowledge of the collective, platonism. Platonism is a study of the metaphysics of inversion, opposition to reality, also known as platonic realism.

Plato is credited with writing a discussion between Socrates, Critias, Timaeus and Hermocrates which is called 'Timaeus'.

On the subject of creation the character Critias says:

> "First, there was The Moon in the orbit nearest the earth, and next The Sun, in the second orbit above the earth; then came the morning star and the star sacred to Hermes, moving in orbits which have an equal swiftness with The Sun, but in an opposite direction; and this is the reason why The Sun and Hermes and Lucifer overtake and are overtaken by each other. To enumerate the places which he assigned to the other stars, and to give all the reasons why he assigned them, although a

> secondary matter, would give more trouble than the primary. These things at some future time, when we are at leisure, may have the consideration which they deserve, but not at present."

Plato's works influenced heavily the medieval concepts of Christianity, Judaism and Islam which merged the mythical and religious elements to a unified story of evolution by the creation of a mathematical construct of time and orbital motion of the planets and hermetic characters. Neoplatonism which emerged in the third century in a similar timeline to the gnostic movement, incorporates the philosophy of the nature of reality, and how the whole is the sum of all components that is a biosphere which is the universe, and through the practice of Theurgy the spiritual goal is to reunite oneself, with the whole transcendental 'One' and ascend to share in the ultimate knowledge of the collective universal consciousness.

Binah Sophia

Sophia

Binnah is the Hebrew term for reason, in the next chapter I explain the Benu bird. Binah is a derivative of this word together with the word 'Sophia', the Greek word for wisdom and from these we get the Cabalistic Judaism and Christian Gnosticism merger to form the goddess Binah-Sophia, wife of God (El) or Yahweh, Binah Sophia make up the Shekinah which means dwelling, this is attributed to the womb and therefore is the mother of God.

Sophia is the goddess of wisdom widely respected amongst many geographical regions and has not been actively maligned throughout history by any religions. She is worshiped today by neopagans and the new age movement, even the Orthodox and Roman Catholic church, Sophia, known as Hagia Sophia (Holy Wisdom), is an expression of understanding for the second person of the Holy Trinity. The unification of enlightenment and wisdom Phosphorus Sophia is a result of Philosophy. Sophia is the mother of wisdom; I believe another name for Perictione mother of Plato

Links to King Arthur

From Greek Mythology we have a link to King Arthur phonetically, Arthurian legend is covered later in this book, but since this phonetic link is part of Greek Mythology the larger body of the work other than the phonetic similarity should be listed here.

Greek Orthodox

In Greek Ortho-dox (Arthur-Dox) of the Eastern Orthordox Church, the word Orthros means early dawn or daybreak. Orthros forms part of early morning religious services, other than that there is not much to expand on, it is purely its relevance to the morning star aspect of Lucifer, but where we find a morning star, there must also be an evening star.

Continuing to Greek mythology which makes this link worthwhile is the character Orthrus.

Orthrus and Cerberus.

Many of the characters in this particular segment share the same attributes so I will just declare a single threaded story but will also highlight some of the repeated symbolism in the characters. Orthrus is a two headed dog in ancient Greek mythology which was tasked with guarding Geryon's Castle, Geryone was a giant monster with one body and three heads, six hands and six feet (totalling 12 Appendages).

Orthrus was brother of the hound of Hell known as Cerberus the three faced (headed) dog that Guards the entrance of Hades. The underworld.

This brother combination would lead us to the consideration that Cerberus is the negatively portrayed *Evening star* character, and Orthrus is more acceptable the *Morning Star* character in this plotline, however this is not the case as Orthrus is charged with guarding the herd of red cattle at Sun-Set.

The red cattle, maybe Taurean influence, sunset seems to indicate the evening star character also, in this tale. Maybe Cerberus and Orthrus in this instance may just be different versions of the story.

Cerberus has three heads, much like the three faces representing the 3-in-1 Holy trinity plotline. Orthrus only has two, but is placed with his master Eurytion rather than alone which is the case for Cerberus.

A phonetic combination of Orthrus and Cerberus, does bring us close to Ouroboros.

It transpires that Orthrus is killed by Heracles as one of his (12) twelve Labours, his legendary tales.

Eurytion with his two faced dog, I consider to be phases of Venus signifying a clear link to The Sun as Orthrus's master.

Eurytion as a name is used for a few characters in Greek mythology, as Greek gods tend to encounter each other in different situations. In one instance he is a Centaur (Human Body and strangely body of a horse) logic would dictate the 'Taur' part would suggest the body of a Bull.

He seemingly is not a nice character and attempts to rape Hippodamia at her wedding to Perithous and is later killed by Heracles.

This leaps to many previously mentioned characters, the rape is defining a pure and virginal mother character, the name Hippodamia, relates to Set (Seths) attempts to disguise himself as a hippopotamus, covered in the next chapter (Egyptian).

In another instance Eurytion is associated with the Herdsmen character which is described also later in the Abrahamic Cain and Abel story. In this Character he is a son of Ares, which if you look up the Greek character Ares on the internet you are instructed not to confuse him with the astrological figure *'Aries the Ram'* because we do not want to corrupt the historical accuracy do we, yet laughingly Ares is one of the TWELVE (12) Olympians in the archaic tradition represented by the Iliad and Odyssey. Ares is often depicted with a dog and a flaming sword, and his father is Zeus, I don't think we need to go any further highlighting the cross-references to this character. On Killing Eurytion in this instance Heracles ceases all the herd, symbolism of the stars being retaken or absorbed by The Suns light upon sunrise. Orthrus is known to sometimes be depicted with one, two or three heads, but as a symbol of renewal and additional link to Ouroboros and Cerberus, is sometimes depicted with a snake tail.

Combining the three animalistic compliments we have

Ort-Horus (horse)
The Cen-Taur (Bull/Horse)
The Serpent (Tail)
Horus-Borus (OuroBorus) the Horse and the Bull and the snake.
The Equine (Horse) **Ox** (Bull)

> ***Borr*** *is Old Norse…which won't come as a surprise by now, means "Son" and is origins of the word "Born", to be infertile you are borren (barren), Celtic Scottish babies are called "Bairns" if they're a pretty child they would be "Bonnie", French Bon means Good (god), November the 5th the end of Samhain in pagan tradition is known as Baal's fire, when we have a Bon-Fire. Traditionally held in Scotland on a high place, called a Ben as in Ben-Nevis. And Ben in Hebrew…you guessed it, means Son.*

Egyptian

There is much to be said regarding Lucifer and his association with Horus, which crosses over several times in other chapters of this book. I thought I would take the opportunity to introduce another Egyptian figure which has a bearing on the Lucifer principles. Since we finished the last chapter on the word *"Ben"*, lets continue.

Bennu (Benu) the bird is a deity from ancient Egypt, and you will have seen hieroglyphs depicting it in the form of a bird. For our purposes it is his association with creation, rebirth and life that is of interest. His predominant symbolistic figure is noted for the raised feathers over its head, this is a symbol of wisdom, the ability for the mind to rise up into a more spiritual plane, the feather in ancient Egypt is used to measure the weight of one's soul, similar to the Cabalistic belief where matter is a tributary of weight on the man's soul, the heavier the soul the further away from ascension and the higher self.

The Greek equivalent of Benu is the legendary Phoenix who most will be more familiar with. A bird who we are told is the essence of fire itself, and one that rises from the ashes as a symbol of rebirth, recreation and renewal. This association was identified by the fifth century BCE Turkish-born historian Herodotus while on a visit to Egypt and comparing the mythos of the creature.

As Luciferians we are soul searchers, we identify with the unique wonderment of self-realisation and the Bennu bird in Egyptian was coined as the Ba of Ra, Ba is our individually distinct divine shape of consciousness and personality, it is our unique presence, although Ba is not confined to living creatures, Ba exists in all things.

Consider if as a child you and your sibling are given identical teddy bears, these bears would have unique Ba's (Bau in its correct plural) to the individual who owns them.

My path as a Gnostic Luciferian is such that we are separated by life from the greater universal consciousness as independent observers, similar to the Neoplatonist's 'The One', a spiritual essence of the collective universe.

The Egyptian belief was not dissimilar, and they believed that upon death the Ba would return to re-join with the 'Ka' in the afterlife. Ka is the spirit or soul more modern esotericism would associate this entity as Chi, my version is the universally collective consciousness. The Egyptians had a more material sense to the Ka than I, and it was to be considered more like the essence of life within the physical body. The Ba is your accumulated individual personality which is road mapped by the material environment. It is not the physical person but the distinguishable person himself.

A point of interest would be to know that the Hindi letter for the Ka is a simple cross + formed in Brahmi (an ancient Indian language one of the earliest forms of writing). Brahmi the language originated in the Central Asia region and in Hindu mythology, Brahmi is goddess learning and power. Brahmi (aka Bacopa) is also a herb which upon consumption has known effects of treating the psychosomatic disorder, reduces stress and improving one's memory. Brahmi is used to treat Alzheimer's disease, anxiety, attention deficit-hyperactivity disorder (ADHD), allergic conditions and irritable bowel syndrome. All things an enlightened person should seek to attain.

Bennu was a self-created at conception and for eternity had the ability to recreate himself over and over again, while not directly a feat attributed to the archetypes associated with

Lucifer the Benu's legend shares many of the Luciferian ideals.

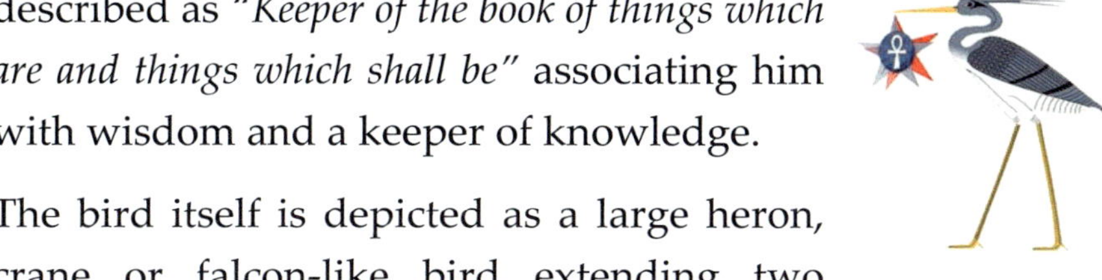

In the book of the dead the Bennu bird was described as *"Keeper of the book of things which are and things which shall be"* associating him with wisdom and a keeper of knowledge.

The bird itself is depicted as a large heron, crane or falcon-like bird extending two feathers above his head, He spends his life creating his own funeral pyre and setting it on fire, from which he is reborn in an eternal and cyclic manner similar to those observed celestially. Its lifespan is said to be five hundred years, which coincided with the Herodotus's claim that the creature lived in Arabia and visited Egypt once every five hundred years upon the death of his father. The Phoenix encased the remains of his father in an egg made of Myrrh, which he had brought to the temple of The Sun.

Horus, who is traditionally aligned with Lucifer, is depicted as having a falcon head. Dr Walter Beltz of Berlin's Humboldt University stated "Some have said that Horus too appeared in the Bennu bird". Horus indeed is iconic of resurrection, Horus's reign was one thousand years and equal to two cycles of the Bennu bird.

The two cycles are possibly significant in the birth cycles of Horus, Lucifer and Jesus. Jesus is always lamented by the prophecy of the second coming of Christ and as mentioned before his reign begins and ends with a Mary character. Mary the Virgin and Mary the Fallen.

In Christian texts, we have the character Mary Magdalene and in this incarnation she is considered to be a prostitute, used and fallen. To complete the thousand year cycle of Horus, Bennu completes two births, one to the pure mother Mary and one to the fallen mother. Potentially also being *'The Whore of Babylon'* a dualistic interpretation of the story 'where there is good, there must be evil, where there is black there is white and where there is night there must follow a day'.

Logically a righteous interpretation must be followed by a notorious incarnation, this is the same for the Christ, and then the Anti-Christ, this simple principle.

However the law of dualism and of that which is Satan is much like the saying the *"Grass is always greener on the other side"*, Satan is that which we are not, Day is on the other side of the world when it is night, yet we accept the beauty and rest we need and lavish ourselves in the glory of its reign. In dualism, evil is the opposite side of our good and although, from the outside perspective of the two juxtaposed positions, we will always perceive ourselves as being good.

On the first cycle Jesus or Horus would be born to *"the virgin"*, on the Second cycle *"the whore"*, however from our perspective the whore will always be the mother that is to come or who was in the past.

Reiterating the above cyclic component of *Mary the Virgin* and *Mary the Fallen*, Lucifer himself appears at both the beginning and the end of the Bible, in Genesis as the tempting snake in the *Garden of Eden* and as *The Dragon* in the last chapter of the New Testament, Revelations.

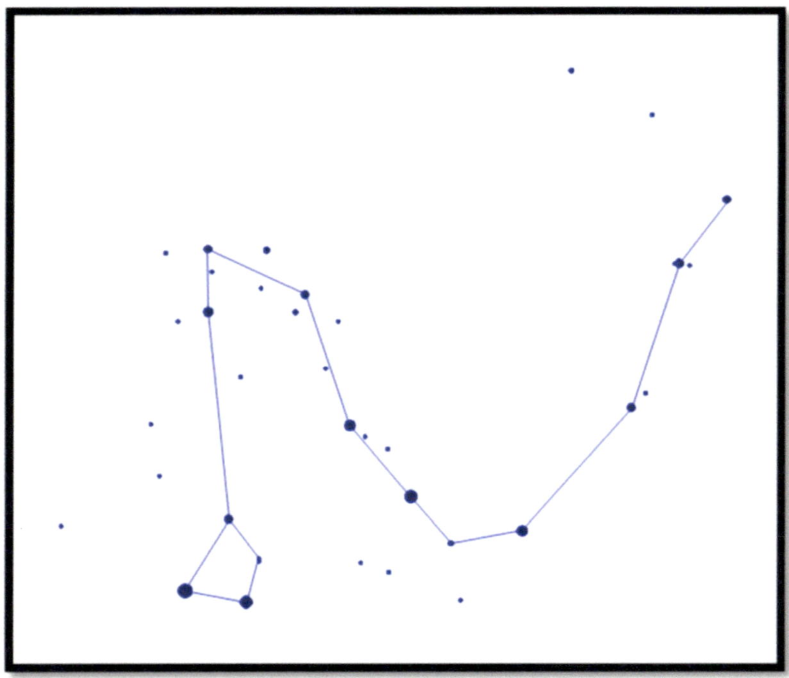

The constellation Draco the dragon and its serpentine nature.

For the time being I don't wish to go into too much detail about the astrological aspects of the characters which will be covered in much greater detail in my forthcoming book ***AstroGenusi***, but Draco exists in the northern hemisphere and is circumpolar which means it is always visible from the northern hemisphere and from 4000 years BC to 1800BC a significant time of writing, for many of the documents we lay credence to today, Draco had a member star called Thuban which was the Polar star at that time and so extremely significant to astral observation. Our current north star is Polaris, Thuban is sometimes also called *The Dragon's Tail* as it resides in the latter quarter of Draco's tail, (third star from the right in the above image) it is also known as Adib. It is due to the earth's axial precession *(its slow wobble)* that shifts over time that it is no longer our pole star, but will be again in about 20,000 years as we are 6,000 years into its 26,000 year cycle, so no time soon.

This is the time of the building of the pyramids and meanwhile over in Egypt the builders of these mega-structures aligned the north passage of the great pyramid to make Thuban perfectly aligned so that it, in theory, would always be pointing at this apparently very static star.

Being the static constellation because logically the earth rotates around its north pole, so if the *North Pole* points towards a constellation the constellation while rotating will not change position, in fact, Draco would appear to rotate with the star Thuban as its pivot from the earth observer. Maintaining its position throughout the night defines him as the king of the night sky as this was considered the centre of the heavens.

The significance of a pole to the Egyptians is visible in all of its most prevalent characters; it signified righteousness, a vertical ascension to heaven. Characters who carried a pole were wise and divinely imbued as rulers; this straight alignment is why we have a correlation between the words 'to rule' as king or queen, and a measuring ruler. They are used to say what is right and correct; they are able to rule on a decision. The measure and the rule are all important and leads us into masonic lore.

Being wise and just they become 'justice' and able to judge and so Thuban was *'Judge of the Earth'* and by Christian doctrine the second coming of the Christ, will be Judgement Day. I can only speculate if that means in 20,000 years when Thuban next regains his seat on the throne of the pole or if it is a shorter term that can be applied to any star in any constellation that occupies the North-Pole spot. If so it has already come along with this current pretender to the throne, Polaris.

Abrahamic (Hebrew)

My hints towards Abrahamic comparisons in the previous sections of this chapter will be brought together in this section I shall jump straight in with Lilith, the dualistic opponent of Eve in the book of Genesis.

The Matronit character Lilith was the mother of the four winds, bearer of disease, illness, death, the whore of Babylon and Adams first wife.

> *"Babylon the Great, the Mother of Prostitutes and Abominations of the Earth."*

In this rotation of worship the female is in her negative polarity, all things have an equal and opposite, she seems to be vilified as the whore instead of the 'mother pure' such as Matatu or later the *Virgin Mary,* although Magdalene still makes an appearance in the New Testament as by this point the astral and celestial definition of the texts we now call the bible is all but lost in the legend; the mythos itself, so men misread it and whether that was intentional or not we will probably never know.

Over the years, the goddess has had many names, Inanna the pure in Suma, Ishtar in Akkad, Annath or Asherah in Canaanite.

The goddess figure would be presented with three dominions Virginity and purity to give birth to a holy and pure son of the gods, later promiscuity, fallen, shamed this is symbolic of the maturity of womanhood by the shedding of the blood or menstrual cycle, the blood would be then attributed to bloodshed or war. These goddesses would nearly always be goddesses of love and war, love would be manifest in both motherly and sexuality and therefore fertility and also war, simply by the bloodshed.

goddess characters in the patriarchal cycle lose all their real significance and become mere wives, consorts, sister or mothers to the gods. Rest assured ladies, this is cyclic and the goddess will rise again and by all accounts very soon, but for the Luciferian we understand that the cycle is symbolic of the flow of energy, every Yin needs it's Yang. We allow those who are not enlightened to believe that strength is aligning yourself with the dominant polarity that is current. We, however, recognise the balance of the whole and abstract ourselves from the revolution and observe its turning.

Lilith is a female demon who flies around the night sky, looking for new-born children to kidnap or strangle, she is particularly associated with the snake or serpent.

In addition to the concept of the cyclic nature of these events you have to consider ideological events at the time. Cultures in very close proximity to each other around the Mediterranean Sea all had their versions of the gods as you have seen above, and while crossover surely exists as does division, particularly if you can use the segregated nature of belief to inspire support for a more military campaign. The Abrahamic or Sumerian counterpart to the Babylonian or Roman version would always be construed as the whore to their virgin, The Satan to their Christ depending on what side of the fence you were standing. Always remember Satan is 'That which we are not'. All beliefs other than your own are Ha-Satan by its true definition rather than that of those who actually choose to pursue a Satan based system, which literally is impossible. Neo-Satanism is more a rebellion using the archetype Satan as a figurehead. Thus, Lucifer is Satan to Christian beliefs. Luciferians on the other hand should not see Jesus as Satan in the same light even though he literally is, as our path is that of enlightenment and the acceptance of these dualistic counterparts as being one and the same is what defines us as being wiser and enlightened.

Lilith had seven daughters

Revelations 12- The Woman and the Dragon

> *[1]A great sign appeared in heaven: a woman clothed with*
> *The Sun, with The Moon under her feet and a crown of*
> *twelve stars on her head. [2]She was pregnant and cried*
> *out in pain as she was about to give birth. [3]Then another*
> *sign appeared in heaven: an enormous red dragon with*
> *seven heads and ten horns and seven crowns on its*
> *heads. [4]Its tail swept a third of the stars out of the sky*
> *and flung them to the earth. The dragon stood in front*
> *of the woman who was about to give birth so that it*
> *might devour her child the moment he was born. [5]She*
> *gave birth to a son, a male child, who "will rule all the*
> *nations with an iron sceptre." And her child was*

snatched up to God and to his throne. [6]The woman fled into the wilderness to a place prepared for her by God, where she might be taken care of for 1,260 days.

[7]Then war broke out in heaven. Michael and his angels fought against the dragon, and the dragon and his angels fought back. [8]But he was not strong enough, and they lost their place in heaven. [9]The great dragon was hurled down—that ancient serpent called the devil, or Satan, who leads the whole world astray. He was hurled to the Earth and his angels with him.

Then I heard a loud voice in heaven say:

"Now have come the salvation and the power and the kingdom of our God, and the authority of his Messiah. For the accuser of our brothers and sisters, who accuses them before our God day and night, has been hurled down.[11]They triumphed over him by the blood of the Lamb and by the word of their testimony; they did not love their lives so much as to shrink from death.[12]Therefore rejoice, you heavens and you who dwell in them!

But woe to the earth and the sea, because the devil has gone down to you!

He is filled with fury, because he knows that his time is short."

> *[13]When the dragon saw that he had been hurled to the earth, he pursued the woman who had given birth to the male child. [14]The woman was given the two wings of a great eagle, so that she might fly to the place prepared for her in the wilderness, where she would be taken care of for a time, times and half a time, out of the serpent's reach. [15]Then from his mouth the serpent spewed water like a river, to overtake the woman and sweep her away with the torrent. [16]But the earth helped the woman by opening its mouth and swallowing the river that the dragon had spewed out of his mouth. [17]Then the dragon was enraged at the woman and went off to wage war against the rest of her offspring—those who keep God's commands and hold fast their testimony about Jesus.*

Here again we see the Bible ending in a birth, as it began with the birth of the universe and a serpent-like in the garden of Eden, the cyclic nature of the Bible reflecting the cyclic nature of astral observation, the book of revelations describing both the fall of the serpent, the fall of the woman and the birth of a new king of the heavens, our current polar star.

Cain (and Abel)

Cain was according to the Old Testament the son of Adam and father of Enoch, you may readily recall the more famous elements of this character by association with his brother Abel. The legend of Cain and Abel is one of the foremost stories that is given as anecdotal of dualism in the Bible and in the Luciferian sense it tells the tale of banishment by god for wrongdoing in the eyes of God after a period of exhalation, much like the rising star then the fallen angel theme that is repeated throughout biblical texts as metaphorical stories.

In the legend Cain was the first 'born' human, that is born of the womb, his mother was Eve, *Father Adam* as mentioned, and this gives him symbolic precedence as being effectively a miraculous child since the concept of creating by procreation had not been broached in the bible or if taken literally, universally since the literal meaning dictates that conception through procreation had not been achieved anywhere until this point, all creatures would also have been pure.

Cain was a crop farmer; symbolism would be dominion over the earth, nature and land. His brother Abel is identified as a shepherd, and so symbolically has dominion over animals and this places him in opposition.

Abel (which in Assyrian literally translates to son) again in dynamic opposition was the first human to die, more duality is exhibited by the stability of the farmer role that is attributed to Cain as a farmer of the land, who sets roots and is steadfast lying in opposition to the nomadic nature of the shepherd who is in motion, free and untethered.

The story lends itself to the morning star and the evening star premise, first born being the morning star, first to die being the evening star. It was believed in these times that the two stars were separate entities, not a single planet Venus. This only came later with some debate on whom clarified the matter, Sumerians it is believed were aware of this, The Greeks found out later by either the spreading of the knowledge or by observation. The story continues that Cain and Abel presented *The Lord* with offerings from their toil, Cain offered produce, and Abel offered a fatted lamb. God it would seem is not vegetarian and 'regarded' Abel favourably for his offerings but did not regard Cain in the same manner, this made Cain angry and resentful towards his brother.

In the Cain and Abel story, much like the afore mentioned 'Horus kills Set, Set Kills Osiris, Horus grows into Osiris' cycle, Cain kills Abel out of jealousy in the same way God condemns Lucifer to his fall for Pride. Surely it must be seen that for God to condemn Lucifer for pride then God exhibits jealousy.

The names Cain and Abel are English renderings of the Hebrew Qayin (קין) and Hevel (הבל) and just to tie up the connection to the Egyptian comparison above, Cain and Abel had another brother Seth (Set).

As punishment for his sins, Cain was forced to drink the blood of Abel and was banished from the land, forever to wander. Cain is now identified as a wandering star. In classic astrology, a wandering star is one of the seven visible planets or moving heavenly bodies, which were The Sun and Moon and the five planets Mercury, Venus, Mars, Jupiter, and Saturn. The word planet comes from the Greek "planētēs" which translates as 'wanderer'.

Taken in the same context that Lucifer, Set, Satan or the Devil are the embodiment of evil by Christian teaching and Cain in folklore being identified as the sinner, and the first murderer in Theological Creationisism and Abrahamic legend, he becomes the Antihero, he symbolises death, evil, sorcery and trickery due to his lying to God over the death of his brother Abel.

The descendent path of Cain became the Cainites, a gnostic sect who venerated Cain as a victim in the same way other gnostic sects venerated Lucifer. The Cainites believe that Cain was a victim of the Demiurge and in traditional Luciferian style when I regard the story of Cain being rejected by god for the inadequacy of his offerings, then you have to sympathise with his dilemma if not his actions. He was by destiny a farmer given dominion over the crops; his work is equal while opposite to Abel's. Yet Abel, in this case, is seen as good and favoured by God with little consideration of people's lot (no pun intended).

The Cainites separated the supreme god from god the creator god who in their version of events 'favoured' the Jews.

This is traditional East, West conflict. The East perceived as Good, creative, *of birth*, The West, due to the rotation of the earth is where The Sun sets and where the stars die or go after their fall from the apex of their epoch. Biblically Cain was banished to the 'Land of Nod' which we now use as a metaphor for sleeping. As patriarchal representation we have the three first meaning Father, First Son Cain and The Holy

Ghost, or the son of death, in Kabbalah the first triad of the twelve which correspond in the Sephirothal Tree to the Crown(fire divine spark), Wisdom (earth, land worker or matter) and intelligence (air or knowledge). Our affiliation with Lucifer means our interest is in wisdom, we are fallen angels, therefore, cast into matter we are earthly, mortal, of the physical plane, sons of Adam. Remember Adam was made of dust and the material makeup of man can be represented by the mind being of the air, higher up in the head (head-ve-n), where his feet are of clay and close to the ground (heel/Hell); we must walk because we are fallen and look up to the sky forever bound to the earth by our feet. This maybe the inspiration for Dante's vision of Lucifer bound to the frozen lake, that which was once liquid is now solid, and his wings from which he could once fly now clipped and made redundant by his imprisoned feet.

Now just to throw in a curveball, in ***Exploring the Divine*** I mentioned how England derives from the land of the angels. Next to England is a small but well-regarded island which lies between England and Ireland called *The Isle of Man.* Adam had three sons; they were the first mortal men bound to earth by their feet. The flag of the Isle of Man is the triskele (or triskelion) which is three legs, emanating from the centre, an ancient pagan symbol.

Taurus-Horus (Hadad)

A Bull-Abel (Ba'al or Bel)

Cain being *Aires* the ram replaces the bull *Taurus* in the procession of astrological ages and becomes the Shepherd of man.

The Cain and Abel story is metaphorical of Jewish belief in their chosen society, Cainites became representative of separation from Hebraic lineage and supportive of Gentile lineage. Because of their adversarial viewpoint to the biblical party line were considered devil worshipers by the more orthodox divisions of biblical scholars. At this point in time, being the first century AD biblical Scholars were far more diverse than we conceive today.

Today we have the Vatican dictating their version for the Christians, and other accepted mainstream Abrahamic descendants such as Judaism and Islam and the debate continues as to who's interpretation is the 'true' one.

This seems to lead to a lot of unnecessary conflicts as the mainstream follow these three main participants and hopefully our social evolution means that one should never entirely wipe out the other, that does not mean that they didn't in the past with heretics such as the Cainites were either destroyed by force or absorbed into other larger organisations.

Cainites became the adversary, Ha-Satan and so have long been regarded as Satanist and patrons of European sorcery and witchcraft.

The First Mourning (Adam and Eve mourn the death of Abel) by William-Adolphe Bouguereau 1888

"The First Morning"

Jesus

Always a source of opinions and controversy which leads to the question "Is Jesus, Lucifer?" I think more directly this should be "Is the Jesus a reworking of the Lucifer Story". To me it certainly seems to be true, at least with my bias towards the astrological basis of Venus being Lucifer, but that is a whole book in itself so I will try to stick more to the written stories of Jesus in comparison with Lucifer.

Jesus said *"I am the light of the world: he that followeth me shall not walk in darkness, but shall have the light of life."* which does indeed sound very much like a trait of Lucifer. A Luciferian's path certainly adheres to the desire to be illuminated, to not walk in darkness. There is no ambiguity about this statement, nobody would for one moment believe this referenced physical light and darkness; it is a direct inference that his followers would be enlightened, it does not promise heavenly reward in the afterlife it clearly says "shall have the light of life."

Mormons claim Jesus and Lucifer were brothers

Joseph Smith, Founder of the Mormons, wrote:

> *"We learn from the scriptures that Lucifer -- once a son of the morning, who exercised authority in the presence of God before the foundations of this earth were laid -- rebelled against the plan of salvation and against Jesus Christ who was chosen to be the Saviour of the world*

> *and who is spoken of as the 'Lamb slain from the foundation of the world.'"*

So clearly he saw the character of Jesus as separate from Lucifer, and the Mormon theology is that Jesus and Lucifer were in fact brothers as all heavenly entities were a creation of the heavenly father, and so without Gods will, Lucifer or Satan for that matter could not have been created, this seems logical from both a theological creationist point of view and an astrological point of view. All phenomena must be a child object of a greater universe, which they are a component of. Brigham Young, second to Joseph Smith in founding the Mormons concurs with our 'Morning Star' version of Lucifer by referring to him as the son of the morning by saying:

> *"Who will redeem the earth, who will go forth and make the sacrifice for the earth and all things it contains?" The Eldest Son said: "Here am I"; and then he added, "Send me." But the second one, which was "Lucifer, Son of the Morning," said, "Lord, here am I, send me, I will redeem every son and daughter of Adam and Eve that lives on the earth, or that ever goes on the earth."*

Referring back to our Cain and Abel story, there is an inference in Mormon teachings that Lucifer and Jesus were Brothers. It can be read to be confirming that the Old Testament version of creation is rehashed in the New Testament and a replication of the story that one son makes an offer to God, as does the other and one is accepted while the other is rejected.

The rejected Lucifer then becomes jealous when God chose Jesus to be 'Our Saviour'. Lucifer was angry and rebelled against the Heavenly Father as told in Revelations 12:79 and Moses 4:34. There is a slight reversal of roles in this case in that Jesus is believed to be the first born of God and, therefore, the older brother.

It is important to remember that to the Mormons we are all spirit children prior to our mortal birth, and that Lucifer became Satan the adversary rather than a character. He too was a spirit child of God. God's spirit children now have to decide whether to follow Jesus or Lucifer. They go on to say "One-third of Heavenly Fathers spirit children chose to follow Lucifer, and they were all cast out of heaven. Lucifer became Satan, and the spirits who followed him became evil spirits, who try to get us to do wrong things. These spirits who followed Satan did not receive physical bodies".

Lilith

Lilith was the goddess Belit-ili, or Belili (Belial) and to the Canaanites, Baalat (baal) the divine lady.

In more obscure texts that the bible edit glossed over but featured in the works 'The alphabet of Ben Sura' circa 900AD Adam became tired of having sex with the animals, sheep, With no offence intended to the inhabitants of the area, it is suggested that this was common practice prior to marital success. So much so that the Old Testament had to declare it a sin (Deuteronomy 27:21) "Cursed is he that lies with any manner of beast".

In our Trinity context, Adam is The Sun, Lilith is the morning Star (first wife) eve is the eve-ning star (second wife). In the tale Adam tried to make Lilith lie beneath him in the act of sexual intercourse or in our interpretation, it is the depiction of The Sun being preceded by Venus, being above him, The Sun rises and dismisses Venus (Lilith, Li) only to be replaced later by Eve (le). In the story Lilith will not subject herself to the demands of man (Adam) considering herself equal as she was made of the same dust, sand, earth or rock material – Earth. Astrologically they appear to rise out of the ground so are created from the earth by the creator god. Whereas Eve was created from a part of Adam, his rib, this is an analogy of Eve becoming the visible form; the light of The Sun, when in the evening The Sun fades, so seemingly is created from a part of the light rather than rising from the earth. Lilith cursed Adam and returned to her home by the sea. in the Book of

Isaiah 34:13–15, describing the desolation of Eden *'lilit'* (Li-Light) is returned to the zoo-logical astrology by being considered as one of the animals in a list of the eight unclean animals with demonic associations. The patriarchal Roman Catholic Church has all but erased all notion of Lilith as it would have to hold the belief that being the angel of the morning, the morning star she would be created before Adam and this would not be acceptable as a goddess figure in the male orientated dogma.

Lilith's home is implied as being the Red sea or River where she is demonised as being a baby stealer and as graphically repulsive as it may sound I believe this red sea connection to be a metaphor for the sad loss of a child, a miscarriage. Lilith did not provide Adam with any children and so the lineage of mankind has to be ended in favour of Eve. Her refusal to be subservient but equal to man has made her iconic of feminism in Neopaganism systems, and I have to concede that indeed she was born first and so would make the goddess figure higher in any hierarchy than man in the form of Adam, but in truth we are talking about a celestial observation, and my luciferian acceptance of my feminine duality makes me confident that the battle for supremacy between any opposing or dualistic attributes means those seeking supremacy are the only weaker or lesser people. We are equal in all measure, race, sex or anything. Adam complained to God who then sent the angels, Sanvi (sanoy), Sansanvi (Sansenoy) and Semangelaf (Semangelof) to retrieve her. A trinity reoccurs, San equals Saint or Sun, so we have Saint Vi (vi-nus) Saint

Sun-Vi, and Se-Angel-af (See-Af(eyelid)) making the all seeing eye and two instances of Venus. The angels were instructed by god to advise her that if she did not return a hundred of her children were to die every day, this is again the obliteration of the stars each day as The Sun rises in a metaphor.

Lilith refused the Angels who threatened to drown her in the sea and she cursed them.

Several accounts then change the direction of Lilith's tale, she either mates with the Arch-Angel Samuel or returns to Eden in the form of the serpent that tempts Eve into eating of the Apple, a transformation tale (shapeshifting).

This version of the bible story is believed to have originated from a story in the epic poem Gilgamesh and the Huluppu Tree an Akkadian work of literature regarding the creation circa 1800BCE. Lilith is one of three creatures who live at the foot of a great Huluppu tree situated in a holy garden of the gods and can be equated to the Norse *Poetic Edda* version of the Serpent Níðhöggr which gnaws at the root of the world tree, Yggdrasil.

Continuing the Abrahamic story, Lilith became a mother figure by fornicating with demons, this in the new testament is the Mary Magdalene, fallen mother in opposition to the purer (Eve) Mary mother of god that occurs in the beginning of the Life of Jesus (his mother and the Vi-rgin) and at his death (Magdalene) wife of Jesus. Where his mother is also present unifying the characters and proving that the authors of the bible knew that *Venus of the Morning* and of the evening were indeed the same celestial body. In the Old Testament she represents the mother of settled agricultural tribes (Canaanites) Cain being the agriculture representations, who resisted the invasions of the nomadic herdsmen, represented by Adam.

The enemy of Cain would be Abel and the great mother is reputed to have drank the blood of Abel, the herdsman, after being slain by the elder god of agriculture, Cain (Genesis 4:11).

Lilith's Red Sea in Hindu is represented by Kali *Ma's Ocean of Blood*. Ka-Li, is also known as 'Dark Mother,' and is the Hindu goddess of creation. Kali serves as the archetypal icon of the birth and death Mother, the same as Mary in the New Testament, simultaneously the womb and tomb, giver of life as well as the devourer of her children.

This creation and destruction paradox is conceptually the self-consuming snake, the creator and devourer of itself, the cyclic creation from destruction, and rebirth an eternal cycle represented by the O'din or O'Dun. Din and Dun in Celtic terms is a circle fortress, or city. A reference to the cyclic universe, the city of God. The Uni-Verse-City. Universe is from the Latin which means 'One-Turned', a reference to the unity of the whole that is all things and the nature of its cycle. Subjectively you are the hub of your universe.

A link exists between Lilith and the ancient Tuskan-Italian religious mythos known as Etruscan, which is rarely mentioned in religious studies due to its overshadowing of the Roman elements from that region. Etruscan mythology which later gave way to Hellenic influences however has a character by the name of Lenith, who possessed no face and waited at the gate of the underworld which seems to me to be a clear parallel to Eve as the Evening Star. Lenith is charged with being a gatekeeper waiting to receive the souls of the dead.

In the Tomb/Womb cycle the underworld gate is often referred to as a yoni, meaning vagina or womb. Yoni (Sanskrit: योनि) - Yoni, is the symbol of the goddess (Shakti or Devi), the Hindu Divine Mother.

The vagina is often depicted by the flower of the Lily, derived from a version of the name Lilith. The Lily has six petals and is often used in esoteric art as a representation in the hexogramatic form.

Admission into the underworld was frequently mythologized as a sexual union and so Lilith is portrayed as the promiscuous type and the Lily plant as a very feminine and sexually poignant flower

The lily or lilu (lotus) was the Great Mother's flower and the Great Mother is represented across many religions Mata, Mary, Cybele, Prajnaparamita, and the wisdom of the Madhyamaka. From this the 'Great mother' with her sexual attributes, we can consider to be'O-Mega' the female equivalent to the Male Al-Pha (EL-Phalus).

Gnostics

The word Gnostic comes from ancient Greek origins by means of the word *knostikos* which translate to 'having knowledge'. In modern times it can be considered similar to the goals of those people who seek a more spiritual life, rather than an academic one. Gnosticism rejects dogmatic concepts of religion, particularly that of the growing Catholic church. Early Gnostics took their teachings from the same middle eastern hermetic scripts as mainstream religions, but they sought to maintain its integrity rather than the forced orthodox regime that later came under secular papal control while remaining an offshoot of that branch of the Abrahamic teachings.

They believed that mankind could achieve a oneness with God, and that man was a purer, more divine form of Gods consciousness manifest in physical material form. There were, in their version of theological history other attempts to create physical entities before mankind but their embodiments failed in such things as compassion and love, and so are to be considered lesser and corrupt versions of man, these were the Demiurge.

The Demiurge was the manifestation of primordial matter, represented by lower and base needs which are in a battle with our spiritual greater self. As such denial of physical presence should be sought by the higher spiritual and godlike self. Rejecting indulgence in all things material.

The Gnostics became celibate, avoided earthly or material possessions and were the foundational influences of many such concepts exhibited by the extremist devout practices today such as Trappist or celibate monks and Buddhists today.

The origin of Gnosticism is debatable but certainly documented sects can be identified between 100CE and 400CE in the Middle East and Asian areas, and although their mystical beliefs predate Christianity it seems to be a generic and adopted component of other belief systems rather than a system in itself. No specific Gnostic texts have been found that predate Christianity, although it has its place in Babylonian history and is heavily embroidered with Neoplatonism.

A great many people believe that Babylon and the Mesopotamian region are the hubs for the birth of civilisation, a misconception which has been taught for many years, but none the less a misconception. We do owe a lot to this region because it holds the earliest documentation of civilisation, all before that must be considered prehistoric, but that should not be interpreted as being the source of the information held within the literature.

Babylon and the middle east did indeed provide us with some of the information, because they are responsible and should be applauded for assembling the knowledge from the known world and were the earliest so far found discovered able to write it down for our perusal, again they deserve great recognition for that. However, the knowledge they recorded was the cumulative efforts of mankind from across the globe.

The Gnostics believed Lucifer to be the light of God, wisdom and enlightenment and that God himself was distinct and unknowable by man in his physical form. Lucifer would show man the light and is a part of reconnecting man with the divine state of pure spirituality. It is in accordance with the concept of Jesus Christs in that 'No man can enter the kingdom of heaven except through Christ' Lucifer in the gnostic sense is this Christ, he is the point of crossing into illumination, that is not to say that all Gnostic Luciferians believe Christ as an interpretation of Lucifer, but many do. Lucifer is the angel of indestructible fire and spiritual guide beaconing salvation and freedom from the Demiurge that binds us to the physical realm, our prison.

The gnostic way was to seek within yourself the liberation of the imprisoned spirit and to know who you truly are, once this state of enlightenment is reached we can return to the greater God-consciousness, which is unknowable while we are bound by the enslaving demiurge.

Neo-Gnostic Luciferians believe that Lucifer is simply a representation of the cognitive knowledge of mankind and his potential, a path to man's apotheosis.

Duality is represented here by the separation of the spirit from the body, the body is effectively the binding of man, created by the Satanic god who imprisoned man in the Garden of

Eden, Lucifer appeared as the snake, a messenger from the unknowable god to remind us of our spiritual origins.

Symbolically Gnostics depict man stood on the serpent. This could either mean that he is lifted by the serpent or as occasionally the serpent replaces man's legs, he could be a grounding representation of the physical being separated from the earth which is seen as the gollum, the earth as an elemental representation of the non-spiritual but fully physical aspect of existence.

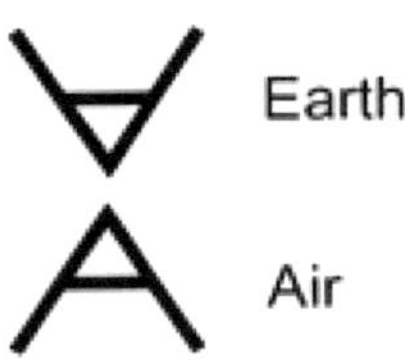

This duality concept gives us the Gnostic opposition to the Earth and the air which if we combine the elemental model symbols for these two elements, which I cover later in more detail, present themselves as the very recognisable mystical symbol, the hexagram. To the Gnostics the universe is divided into three kingdoms *The Earthly Cosmos* is physical and contains the underworld, a realm that is not underground but within the material earth itself, it too is unknowable and satanic as it is the place where we are not. The lower dimensions of man.

The Intermediate kingdom where we reside being a component of the duality between the lower realm and the upper, it is the surface of the earth, the transitional or juxtaposed existence, the Sophia which is illumination contained within the earth. Lastly *The Kingdom of God* which contains two spheres of existence, the outer sheer being the unknowable god and the inner being the son of god.

Norse

I doubt you will find much elsewhere that associates any of the Nordic gods with Lucifer or luciferian concepts. But I believe there is one, and I believe that much of the mythos is once again another version of that reoccurring cyclic astral story.

Lucifer, I hope you will now agree is an astrological deity, he is lord of light and heavily associated with Venus and the concepts that surround it, in terms of parentage relating to father, son, brother, life, death cycles.

The Nordic legends are influenced by the northern European culture, the stories are heavily influenced by the cooler climate experienced in the northern hemisphere, but still, the people were like all others, they were heavily dependent on astronomy and the legends they conceived were a tool to interpret and record astrological science in their own way.

The Vikings used only stars to navigate the seas around the cold artic areas of the North Sea, around Britain, Iceland and the Scandinavian regions. They had their own spiritual universe which was based on an ash tree called Yggdrasil pronounced ig-dra-zil or eeg-dra-zil. This metaphysical tree whose branches spanned worlds and dimensions is the Nordic version of the kabbalisc "*Tree of Life*" or Etz haChayim. It is not important nor do I ever believe we will know which of the legends came first? And that is just two of the many "Tree of life" stories that exist in almost all cultures. Mesopotamians had the sacred Haoma, which bore all seeds.

The Egyptians and Assyrians trees were represented as branches between spheres of existence and no doubt lead to or was a part of the Kabbal's evolution, more oriental religions had trees such as Sadratu'l-Muntahá which was the manifestation of god, Bhuddists have the Bodhi tree which Budda sat under to attain enlightenment, and you see a similar theme between them all.

It is reasonable to question history as I did with the story of Plato, when even in modern times legend influences historical context. You see the legend of Sir Isaac Newton, who became enlightened on his theory of gravity while sat under an apple tree.I have no doubt Isaac Newton existed, and that he conceived the question of gravity being related to mass. But if this enlightening legend stolen from the legend of Bhudda is ascribed to people who lived only three hundred years since, what chance have we of finding out the true nature of those that existed two to six thousand years ago.

> *Point of interest, Sir Isaac Newton was born on the 25th of December (Same as Jesus apparently) in 1642 and Died approaching Easter time on March 31st in either 1726 or 1727. As well as gravity he is known for the dispersion of light through a prism so he was indeed a bringer of the knowledge of light.*

There is a sense within man that to find the origin of religion we find ourselves closer to the truth of god. But rather than claiming which version of belief came first, it is more important to try to find out what they were saying? And most of all why these stories seem to resonate across the entire earth? Did one culture present this complex, multidimensional metaphysical explanation of a universe both within and without man, or is this concept encoded into core beliefs, and why are we moving away from it? Or did some great astrological and environmental event actually occur, that changed the path of man. Finally why is the cycle of Venus and The Sun so important to it?

Yggdrasil consisted of nine worlds separated on its branches across three levels, there is much more to it than that, but that is not within the remit of this book.

The earthly realms were in the middle of the tree and they were Midgard, Jotunheim and Muspellheim.

Their higher and heavenly realms were Asgard, Vanaheim, and Alfheim and lastly the lower levels or underworlds were Svartalfheim, Niflheim and Hel.

If you are familiar with Tolkien's novels such as *The Lord of The Rings,* then this fantasy story has been heavily influenced by the Nordic legend. Midgard, Jotunheim and Muspellheim are like a Middle-earth with lands of humans, dwarves, elves and giants, each have their role to play and racial attributes that define their character.

Norse mythology does have many crossovers with the other middle-eastern concepts I have described in this book, there are the equivalent primordial elements but these are represented as lands rather than as personified gods or spirits. Muspellheim is the land of fire probably identified by the volcanic regions of the Nordic realms; Niflheim is the land of ice, the Polar Regions as we see them today, but historically were more widespread due to the ice age which would have covered this entire region.

These two primordial elements have in Norse mythology always existed but they were surrounded by the void which separates them, the void is called Ginnungagap.

Nifliem would be the element of water, but due to the cold and harsh northern climate they lived in, Ice would rightly be considered the extreme opposite to fire, rather than water as considered by the more equatorial cultures who would have experienced very little in the way of ice.

The Norse culture is lovingly brash like historic tales of Vikings, they were bold and honourable people, and they took what was needed and were happy to die, fighting for their place. Their spiritual ethos doesn't pander to the higher concepts of other mystical beliefs and so creation is explained rather humorously blunt, which is typical of northern Europeans still today.

Where fire and ice met, they formed water and steam which flowed from the void creating the sleeping water giant Ymir. In a cosmic steam room the sweat of his arm pits created male and female as a concept of opposition rather than an attribute of people at this point. In his sleep his feet began to mate and have offspring in the form of a son. This legend begins the Norse story of creation.

A beautiful story so far, I'm sure you will agree. But there is hidden in this story many parallels to Kabbalistic beliefs. We have a tree of life, we have the body, separated into left and right sides as oppositions, male and female. We have flowing of energies in the form of sweat, and you must remember sweat is a result of toil and is therefore honourable to this industrious region. We have the mating of the feet which is an interpretation of the gnostic Demiurge associating the feet with the earth to form matter, directly opposed to the higher spiritual self of the mind from which the energy has flowed.

While sleeping Ymir the giant was nourished by the teats of a great cosmic cow, this is equivalent to Nut or the Milky Way. The association with the cosmic entity being described as milk is quite a remarkable coincidence, in fact it in my mind cannot be a coincidence at all. Even in Greek mythology Amalthea was a goat who raised Zeus, while he suckled on her breast milk.

Auðumbla was licking the ice which in three days formed the first Aesir (pronounced Ice-Ear) Gods that had human form, this entity was called Buri, who went on to have three sons Odin, Vi and Ve.

To me Odin is Omega (meaning the great O) or The Sun. In Norse mythology he is king of the gods, separate from a creator God or the primordial god which is similar to gnostic beliefs. Vi and Ve are the morning and the evening star

(Venus). Vi-Nus, Ve-Nus, Nus is sun backwards and so is opposing The Sun making him the adversary or Anti-Christ so some.

The three sons, fell onto Ymir killing him. Here we have the astrological rise and fall, into the sea. From the earthbound perspective to the east where The Sun would rise was what we now call Russia.

This is both a recurring story and also a tale of fire meeting ice and melting it destructively. The story continues that so much blood flowed from Ymir that it killed all the ice Giants, filled the seas and rivers, this is a biblical proportion flood, in which all the Ice giants died, except for one who floated to safety (Noah?). The story continues of how Odin and his brothers then gruesomely chop up Ymir using his body parts to create all sorts of things such as teeth into rocks, brains into clouds and his blood formed the seas.

I believe this to be an accurate tale of the end of the Ice age. The ice that was the body of the sleeping Ymir retreated and was melted by the effects of the global climate change caused by The Sun, and his two brothers Vi and Ve morning star and evening star, the land underneath this mile deep polar drift, would reveal, rocks, mountains, rivers and seas.

His skull made the dome of the sky and it was held up by four dwarves created from the maggots that were feeding on the corpse of Ymir.

Odin and his brothers, were strolling upon the shore and one day they came across two trees an ash and an elm and moulded them to form a man and a woman. Here we have the story of Adam and Eve (or Lilith) moulded from that which is already on the earth instead of creation from nothing, which God the creator would be able to do. These characters were called Ask and Embla, *A and E.* And they were granted the land of Midgard to themselves and their descendants. In the same way Yahweh granted Eden to Adam and Eve.

The four pillars of creation. They are so named because the gas and dust are in the process of creating new stars - taken by the Hubble telescope in 1995.

In Norse legend there is adversary characters. There is Jörmungandr enemy of Odin and Thor.

THE PUNISHMENT OF LOKI.

Jörmungandr, the serpent who winds around the earth eating his own tail, like Ouroboros or more likely the trajectory of The Sun, *the head of Ouroboros*, circling the earth from the observer's point of view, legend has it that if it ever stopped eating its own tail ,the end of the cycle, then the world would end. Jörmungandr was cast out by throwing him into the sea. Thor, Odin's son is foretold as ultimately killing Jörmungandr in their last battle at Ragnarok, but he will not live out his life as a hero, instead he will die by walking nine paces and falling due to a bite containing Jörmungandr's poison.

Classically a tale reiterating the cycle of killing one, then taking revenge on another, father and son.

We can follow the descendants of the great O' (Odin) himself down to the introduction of Baldur (Baldr) the Norse god of light, and most closely related to the Lucifer character for this region.

Here below we have a version of the tale of Baldr's death translated by Broedur from the *Pros Edda* a 13th century Norse work of literature, which together with the Poetic Edda, it comprises the major basis of Scandinavian mythology.

'The second son of Odin is Baldur, and good things are to be said of him. He is best, and all praise him; he is so fair of feature, and so bright, that light shines from him.'

Baldr is known primarily for the legend of his death. Baldr dreamt of his own death and Frigg his mother shared those dreams, this formed the prophecy and so Frigg made a deal with every object in the realm. She made them vow never to harm Baldr, sadly she omitted to strike the deal with mistletoe, and a plant traditionally used in Europe at Christmas time as part of the Christmas decorations. The full etymology of the word "Mistletoe" is unknown but I do have a theory that follows.

"Mistle" I believe is what we nowadays call 'missile' which comes from the Latin meaning suitable for throwing, the "toe" part has been identified as being from the Old English word "tān" which means twig. Combine we have the word *Missile Twig,* (spear) and here is why I think this is relevant.

Loki hated Baldr and when he heard that mistletoe had not made the pledge he fashioned a spear made of the plant and rushed to where the other gods played games with Baldr, being immune to harm from all things in the world due to the vow, they took sport in throwing things at him and laughed as he went uninjured.

Loki handed the blind god Höðr, Baldr's brother the deadly spear of mistletoe, who then inadvertently killed him although he threw it at him believing he would be unhurt. A story which recites the spear of destiny's place in Christian texts, and in Egyptian texts it is a spear that Horus uses to kill Set. Set appeared in the form of a hippopotamus and hippopotamus is symbolic because of the eyes appearing over the body of water while the body of the creature is below the horizon waddling.

In a vowing revenge Odin impregnated a goddess from the east (an East-Star if you like) and miraculously gave birth to Váli who grew to adulthood in a single day. This 'single day' is significant. Váli is Baldr's and Höðr's brother, he takes revenge on Höðr.

This is again the exact story of Horus, Set and Osiris a child, grows to a man (Horus to Osiris) and kills (Set) in a single day. Höðr's is almost the same word as Horus although in this story he plays the character Set, being the blind god, as sun sets or the eye of Horus, goes out when it gets dark.

Váli much like Ve and Vi makes up that which is visible and *vi-able* pertaining to light, Váli is Venus the star of the morning, who grows into the full sun, effectively as The Sun rises it obscures the morning star, conceptually he grows into adulthood. The revenge for the death is a *váli-ant* thing to do.

The word Baldr etymologically has many definitions; Latvian "Balts", Lithuanian "Baltas" meaning white, pure or good. In Anglo Saxon or *Angel-Saxon* he is called "Baldag" which means "Bal" day or deity. A ball is a sphere or a bull. So we have the whole sphere, sun, day, and deity connection.

Baal, who I go into detail with more later on means Lord in Phoenician culture he was an idol and is accepted by distinguished scholars that Baal or Bel as he is called is undoubtedly The Sun, but is also associated with Jupiter and our old friend Venus.

In a similar way to the crossover of Venus of the morning and Venus of the evening, Baal in Syria had a brother or pseudonym called Hadad which means 'smith' who was a storm god much like Thor, he was responsible for storms and rains, his symbol was a bull and is often depicted with a beard and a horned helmet like the misconception of Viking helmets which could well be what influenced this imagery. In one hand he holds a club, the other a lightning bolt. He is god of rain and agriculture which ties him to the biblical Cain figure.

There was conflict between El (God supreme) and Ba'al (Hadad) just like that between God and Lucifer, so El sent one of his sons called 'Yamm', which means sea, to take Baál from his throne, later there is a battle with a sea serpent called Lotan (Leviathan).

In other accounts there is a feast to which Mot (Mort or Death) is invited, but Mot gets offended by the offering of bread and wine (agriculture) as his preference is flesh and blood, much like the favour of God shown to Abel and the rejection of Cain by Yahweh in the bible story.

My point is, that they are taking the one to one relationship of a God, identifying it with a single planet or star and so this constant mismatch of who or what one God represents is thrown into complete chaos with these ideas. From the astrological point of view he, the god in question is rightfully to be named according to the relationship and position of a combination of these celestial entities not a solitary object.

Arthurian

We begin Arthurian legend in the 5th century CE, unsurprisingly around the same time that St. Augustine first brought Roman interpreted Christian teachings to the lands of northern Europe. Arthurian legend is shrouded in mystery and magic, but despite historians having an excellent grasp of the ordinance of English monarchies and political events around this time, the legend of Arthur remains a source of controversy. If all my previous interpretations of Gods, heroes, prophets and mythos holds true when being applied to geographical legend then this is a plausible to associate this legend equally with the others in portraying the Venus, Sun cycle.

Our story begins with Uther (Uthyr in original spelling) Pendragon, the father of the legendary King Arthur who defeated the Saxons. Uther is unashamedly similar in pronunciation to the Norse god Thor, U-thor and there is no confirmed record of a father to Uther although the surname Pendragon is believed to be derived from the name ben-dragon 'Ben' in root Hebrew means *'son of* or *heir of'* so he would be Uther, son of the dragon (dragon can also be considered inclusive of the word serpent).

Since this is Celtic legend historians claim it means chief, however in true Celtic Scots it would mean *'High'* and Wikipedia claim that "The name was misinterpreted by Geoffrey of Monmouth in the Historia to mean "dragon's head."

I think this is very arrogant of modern day historians, it certainly ties in with the representation of The Sun on its perceived trajectory of circling the earth represented by the Ouroboros symbol. Of course they are approaching the subject from a historical evidence point of view so they try to present accuracies that are terrestrial and earthly whereas my perception is astrological in its bias, I think this was Geoffrey's interpretation too.

U'ther's bloodline has connections to being of Roman descent possibly from the line of Constantine. I am alleging that he is possibly a disputed king but using the legend/god association that has been previously applied in the past to pharaohs and emperors again to bolster the story of the man. This begins early by simply examining the name, Uthyr, or the 'other' O-Thor which gives association to the 'great O', the omega and The Sun of the serpent. Thor's father was O'din. So following the theme in all other cases we start looking for brothers, fathers, battles where one brother defeats another, slays a serpent, carries light, is favoured over a another brother and possibly born to a virgin or pure mother, fed milk from a cow, bulls etc. You should have the theme by now.

Most of what we know about Uther is written by Geoffrey of Monmouth in his *Historia Regum Britanniae* (History of the Kings of Britain). In which Uther has a brother called Ambrosius Aurelianus whose name means food of the gods. Uther went into battle with his brother and won, succeeding him to become King of Britain.

Bizarrely Uther tricks Lady Igraine, the wife of his enemy Gorlius by employing the magician Merlin into disguising him as Gorlius, Uther then sleeps with her and she becomes pregnant with the illegitimate heir to the throne, Arthur. This is comparable to Lucifer's ascension and pride parable and is a story of a woman who conceives while remaining true, in this case she believed she was sleeping with her husband Gorlius.

Other accounts claim that Lady Igraine's husband at this point was already dead and so legitimises Arthur's later claim to the throne. Cyclically the story of illegitimate birth is repeated when Arthur sleeps with his half-sister and sires Mordred (Mot, Mord) who is eventually responsible for killing Arthur at the battle of Camlann.

The legend of Arthurs conception relates to U'ther being a shapeshifter, this is not the first occurrence of this term, as in our other legends Set turns into a hippopotamus in his shapeshifter story.

Historian opponents to the Arthurian legend point out similarities to an ancient Celtic God legend called Hengist and Horsa (AKA Hors (Horus)). These Anglo-Saxons of Germanic origins were brothers who lead the armies that conquered Britain and first established the region called Kent as a kingdom.

Hengst and Horsa were mercenaries who served the then king Vortigern.

Another association we have to King Arthur and his connection to The Sun , Venus of the morning and Venus of the evening scenario comes from the Celtic legend of Hoggs – Queens wake, which is believed to be a story of Mary Queen of Scots and her return to rule Scotland from France in the mid sixteenth century. The poem published in 1813 was a huge success and was subject to many polished revisions to make it more palatable the Georgian consumers.

It reads.

King Arthurs sons o' merry Carlisle
Were playing at the ba (ball)
And there was their sister burd (bird) Ellen
I' (in) the midst amang(amongst) them a' (all)
Child Rowland kicked it wi' (with) his foot
And keppit(kept it) wi'(with) his knee
And aye as he played, out o'er(over) them a' (all)

O'er the kirk(church) he gar'd(watched) it flee
Burd Ellen round about the aisle

To seek the ba' has gane (gone)
But she bade(tried) lang, and aye langer
And she came na(not) back again.
They sought her east, they sought her west,
they sought her up and down
and way were the hearts in merry Carlisle
for she was nae gait(pathway, tracks) found.

To me this is the story of Baal (ball) the brother kicking the ball, the sister seeking to retrieve it and being lost in the underworld or elf kingdom as the poem goes on to suggest. The child Roland (son of Arthur), the brother then goes to seek his sister in the underworld and overcomes the king of Elfland, killing all he meets along the way. And recovers her.

The killing of all others is simply the obfuscation of stars as The Sun rises much like the falling angels joining Lucifer, Roland is The Sun, going to rescue Venus in the evening. The church (kirk) is the kingdom of heaven, Ro-Land is the royal land as Roy is a northern word derived from Roi meaning king, Roy-Al is the King (al) or God.

Ellen (Helen) is a Dutch, English name but of Greek roots and is derived from the word Helios, meaning bright or shining one.

Interestingly King Arthur is associated with the ancient English town of Carlisle which is located on the Scottish-English border and since it is capitalised in the poem we must understand it to mean the location of Carlisle whose name was originally the Roman Luguvalium meaning Stronghold of Lugus, Lugus also means Light or Brightness.

Lugus was a Celtic God depicted as having three heads or faces similarly representing the holy trinity. Lugus the Celtic deity is believed to the principle behind the name of the Scottish borough of Lothian which includes the City of Edinburgh (Eden-Borough (Odin-burgh)) the capital city of Scotland and home of the Scottish rite of freemasonry. Edinburgh Derives its name from Dun Eidyn, which in the 5th century was a part of the Old north of Britain known as Gododdin celtically written as Guotodin (Goat(Good,Gut) Odin).

Loth (loath), meaning hostile, hateful [before 900; Middle English loth, lath, Old English lāth, c. Old Saxon lēth, Old High German leid, Old Norse leithr], Edinburgh has an area called Leith. In Greek Mythology Lethe(Λήθη (Lḗthē)) is the Daughter of Eris, She is one of the four rivers that flow through Hades where the souls of the dead would drink to forget their lives, Celtic Leet or Leeth (lyth) means River or flowing water. Since we are now dealing with a female character in Eden which is negatively portrayed we have a clear phonetic association to Li-Lith (el Lith).

Arthur, A- Thor, Artorious, Horus, Ataurus

Brother Sir Kay, French Kes Kes-Astral (Kestral)

Cia in Celtic (rejoice) Scottish fire (Kia)

Father Uther –U Thor (the Other (Great O' Thor))

The Last Sleep of Arthur in Avalon by Edward Burne-Jones 1891c

Zoroastrian

And so left until last in this chapter is the oldest recorded incarnation of Lucifer, but this this more than an incarnation, this is the revelation of who Lucifer is. The cumulative versions hereto listed point to an astrological interpretation of Lucifer and the astrological origins and observations that we have today which although diluted and deranged into all the known religions of the world stem from a mystic sect of people from Persia and the study of Zoroastrianism.

Mithra, the all seeing eye of truth, Mithra, (mi-tra (who-doorkeeper)) pronounced 'Mee-Rar', guardian of the harvest and the waters, is both male and female. It is the duality of one, the two opposing entities, equal but opposite in all; the two that become one. You are Me-Rah, the light, reflective rays of light that exist within the soul, within the 'mirror'. The ultimate left hand path, you raise your right hand, your reflection raises its right. Your reflection always opposes your entrance into the mirrored world. You are God.

The book of Genesis states *"And God created man to his own image: to the image of God he created him: male and female he created them."*

Zoroastrianism is attributed to a character called Zoroaster, I think we have covered enough evidence that these ancient characters attributed with such things are often not genuinely the case, however for the purpose of comprehensiveness Zoroaster was born approximately 530BC in the area now known as Iran and the regions of Mesopotamia, birthplace of writing, and so we come full circle to where we were early in the book, this does not prove the origin of these beliefs, only the oldest records of it that we can interpret.

We can thank the Zoroaster for our *Zo-Dei* (zodiac), you may have heard the saying "it is easier for a camel to pass through the eye of a needle than a rich man to enter the kingdom of heaven" all sorts of rumours have been propagated as an explanation for this bizarre statement, let me explain. This is a mis-translation from a Zoroastrian saying, when the storyteller is referring to themselves or people of their faith. The misconception being the proto-Indian translation of Ustra (which means camel), the Zoroastrian who's gnostic faith believes as I, that we are separated parts of the collective that is the great one god. A Zoroastrian refers to this great god as Astro, being both himself, the microcosm and the universe. Therefor it is easier for 'me' or 'the universe' to pass through the eye of a needle.

Zoroaster emphasized the freedom of the individual to choose right or wrong and the individual responsibility for one's deeds. Your will is the whole of the law.

The Peacock Angel Tawsi Melek

Yazidis are a linked religious order to Zoroastrianism whose people are primarily in the Middle East but have a high number in northern Europe, particularly Germany, they have Kurdish origins. They claim theirs to be the oldest religion in the world and there is nothing to prove otherwise, it certainly shares roots with the Mesopotamian beliefs, and these nomadic people could easily have brought it to the area, as well as taken it away.

Tawsi Melek, is known as the *"Peacock Angel"* or *"Peacock King,"* and is the primary deity of this religion although not the highest ranking, much like Christianity, worship is through the subordinate and creator God rather than direct to the supreme god who cannot be known. To the Yazidis Tawsi Melek is the true creator and ruler of the universe, and that all other religions are a spinoff of Yazidis belief. He is represented by the peacock, but is able to manifest himself in any way as master of light and he is responsible for all good and bad in people.

At the beginning of time the supreme god created Tawsi Melek as his first and foremost creation, he was light, he was an emanation of gods will, and was there to allow the unseen god a method for his administration of the universe.

Tawsi Melek is the conceptual and manifested representation of the infinite Supreme God which cannot be known by man as it is beyond his ability to conceive, much like my void at the beginning of this book. The supreme God then went on to produce more emanations totalling seven including Tawsi Melek. These can be conceived as the then seven known planets or the more ethereal and spiritual concept of the seven colours of the rainbow. Tawsi Melek is oversear of the other six angels known as 'the great Angels' and so the great angels were originally a part of Tawsi Melek,; luminosity if you like as master of the Hue. Tawsi Melek became associated with the colour blue, because this is the colour of the sky and the heavens and first on the scale of prismatic colours.

This Heptagram is adopted by nearly all Abrahamic and creationist theory, the seven days of creation, seven planets, seven angels, seven colours and seven is a phonetic anagram of Venus (venes).

The Yezidis have their holy book which is called Meshefê Re, again phonetically we have "Mesiah Ra" which describes the universe in its primordial state as a pearl and even goes on like my opening passage to describe it as the stuff of all the universe as a molten mass which was then exploded by gods into what we now term 'The Big Bang' which heralded the seven days of creation.

> *"The first day which He (the Supreme God) created was Sunday. On that day He created an angel whose name was 'Azra'il. This is Melekê Taus, who is the greatest of all.*
>
> *On Monday He created the Angel Darda'il, who is Shaikh Hasan.*
>
> *On Tuesday He created the Angel Israfil, who is Shaikh Shams.*
>
> *On Wednesday He created the Angel Mika'il, who is Shaikh Abu Bakr.*
>
> *On Thursday He created the Angel Gibra'il, who is Sagad ad-Din.*

On Friday He created the Angel Shimna'il, who is Nasir ad-Din.

On Saturday He created the Angel Nura'il, who is Yadin [Fakhr ad-Din].

And God made Melekê Taus the greatest of them."

The book then continues to describe a scientific description of the creation of the earth from the remnants of the universe, how it was hostile and volcanic eruptions and earthquakes. It was Tawsi Malek who then visited the earth and calmed the earth, blessing it with life. He flew around the globe blessing every part of it.

I think we can view this description as the earth centric view of The Sun, but more importantly the knowledge predating Newton's discovery of light being made up of many colours. The Yezidis were clearly referencing this in hermetic texts five thousand years ago.

Man was created next by all the Great Angels. The first human was created by all the Seven Great Angels, each of whom endowed him with one of his physical senses. One gave him an ear, one a nose, one a mouth, etc. But the first human was a lifeless heap without a soul, so Tawsi Melek transmitted the breath of life into him and thus Adam was created. Here we have a hermetic text that actually identifies The Sun as an emanation of god as their book states that Tawsi Melek then pointed Adam towards The Sun and told him that there is something much greater than himself and that each day he should pray to The Sun as representative of the supreme god and that Tawsi Melek's special day is The Sun-Day.

Tawsi Melek then told Adam of the prayers that he must speak, that they would be distributed amongst 72 Languages, one for each of the 72 sons and 72 daughters who would populate the 72 regions or countries of the Earth. *The Peacock Angel* then informed Adam that if he and his descendants remained steadfast in righteousness that they would eventually see and know the supreme god personally. In the meantime, Tawsi Melek would be their protector and teacher even while residing in another dimension.

By many of the mainstream religions Yezidi belief is associated with devil worship, particularly in Islam where he is associated with 'The' Devil called Iblis or Shayṭān one of the origins of the word Satan. Of course this is ironic since we clearly see the evolution of a core belief system here to the Abrahamic doctrine. It is particularly sorrowful from our enlightened viewpoint as we should be embracing these religions, and working together so we can find out the truth of the spiritual man.

Phonetically we can establish a link here with Moloch, Milcom or Molek particularly with his pseudonym of *Melekê Taus* as listed in the above quotation from the Meshefê Re. Phonetically we have the words Molek-Taurus representing

Semitic מלך m-l-k, a Semitic root meaning 'king' who is associated with very costly sacrifices such as that of your own children.

Jeroboam Offering Sacrifice in front of the golden calf. Jean-Honoré Fragonard (1732–1806)

The story, is I believe the 'Moses' story which in modern Christian interpretation, includes the sacrifice of his child to go, although he did not go through with it, and during his absence the Israelites created the *Golden Calf*. There are many classical pictures painted by the great artists of the *Golden Calf*, none of them contain The Sun in the background, Molek was absent, and so this idol was created, Moses returned condemning the Israelites for creating an icon of god.

Moloch appears in the Hebrew of 1 Kings 11:7

Then did Solomon build a high place for Chemosh, the abomination of Moab, in the hill that is before Jerusalem, and Molek, the abomination of the Sons of Ammon.

And In Milton's Paradise lost:

"First Moloch, horrid King besmear'd with blood of human sacrifice, and parents tears, though, for the noyse of drums and timbrels loud, Their children's cries unheard that passed through fire

To his grim Idol. Him the Ammonite worshipt in Rabba and her watry Plain, in Argob and in Basan, to the stream of utmost Arnon. Nor content with such Audacious neighbourhood, the wisest heart

Of Solomon he led by fraud to build his Temple right against the Temple of God on that opprobrious Hill, and made his Grove the pleasant Valley of hinnom, tophet thence

And black gehenna call'd, the Type of Hell."

Moloch is depicted as the Bull, Bel, Baal and interestingly here the root word comes into play of Ball as Molek is where we get the word Molecular, on a similar vein Adam (ammon) is also atom.

Paradise Lost Alexandre Cabanel

Lucifer and the Illuminati.

Before I start with Luciferianism as a concept for those of you that are new to the subject, I will give a brief description of two sectors of the philosophy which translates into many occult and spiritual practices too. For those that are already informed I assure you this will be brief.

There are two spheres, LHP and RHP. It's difficult to pinpoint the less obvious differences between the two. With ideas of spirituality there is no black and white and nowhere is this more evident than with Luciferianism which rides the cusp of the wave between all things. There are generic attributes to the terms RHP and LHP in occult faith systems however, this dichotomy does not always cross over between the various faiths or philosophies.

I believe you must decide for yourself, your take on what constitutes an RHP or LHP

Generic terms would place Luciferian as LHP by default thus assigning it attributes such as being morally unbound, dabbling in black arts, sacrifices, etc. this is not the case.

LLHP (Luciferian Left Hand Path)

Subscribers to this version of the philosophy tend not to believe in a *greater entity such as a god, but that we are gods over our dominion, we control our world around us and by taking advantage of the knowledge we are without bounds and create true freedom and success.

In other occult systems LHP is linked to black magic, not so much in Luciferianism, it is linked more to self-progression in the material sense.

*A subset of LHP also includes *Theistic Luciferians* who perceive Lucifer as a personified deity.

LRHP (Luciferian Right Hand Path)

Is usually ascribed to deity based faiths and as such is not commonly found within the realm of Luciferianism belief, however as I hope this book explains, it is the belief that rather than being god of our own dominion we are a part of God and try to attain mastery of our dominion by channelling this power.

The moral code is principally 'what you do to others you do to yourself' since the belief is that we are all a part of the greater consciousness', we are each other manifested as isolated individuals for the period of our lifespan.

In other occult systems RHP is linked to white magic, not so much in Luciferianism, it is linked more to self-progression in the spiritual sense.

It is easy to switch between the two, both methods of practice are the same, the only difference is the way you rationalise yourself. You are either a god or part of God; you become powerful and successful in the material world, or you seek enlightenment for the sake of it. The lines, however, are grey, one does not exclude the other.

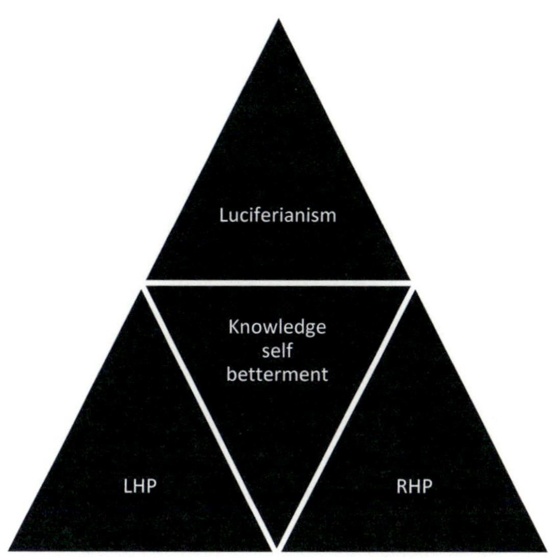

Lucifer was the first and most glorious creature of God according to accounts dating back to the Old Testament. He was also known as the son of dawn or the rising sun. Which is comparable to the descriptions of both 'Jesus Christ' and 'The Egyptian God Horus'.

In ***Exploring the Divine***, I went into greater detail aligning the worship of Horus to the later attributes accredited to the Christian son of God, Jesus. The religious system known now as Christianity existed long before the approximate two thousand years ago that we attribute to the birth of Jesus Christ under many different names and in many different regions of the earth, it is effectively sun worship, if you are of Christian faith and this feels uncomfortable to your faith, then maybe I can placate you with the thought that the faith existed in the form of prophecy long before Christ was made of man, in the words of St. Augustine "What is now called the Christian religion, has existed among the ancients and was not absent from the beginning of the human race". It doesn't matter what name it is given or the age, what matters is that you understand the truth. In this chapter I will be focusing on the Light Bringer, the common element in nearly all gods is this child of the one true God being associated with the rising Sun, the *Risen Son* or first generation of God's offspring.

Segueing back to my opening chapter God said "Let There Be Light" this is a seminal part of Christian worship, most Christians don't really claim to know much of Bible passages, but one thing they will know is the importance of that quote, as it is the one quote almost every Christian will be confident is in the book of Genesis. This specific line identifies the first action or will of God as claimed and recorded and is not disputed by any factions.

Previous biblical descriptions talk of an already existent void, darkness, depths and worlds without substance. However, the first purported action of God is the creation of light. This can be taken as either the entity of optical light on the electromagnetic spectrum in general or it can be taken from a very Earth-centric point of view as a description of the ignition of our local star, The Sun. As Jesus says in John 18:12 "I am the light of the world". Clearly the light of the world and *Son of God* is intended to be a respectful worship of The Sun in heaven. Created as the first child of God or his first action.

If then Lucifer was the first and most glorious creature of God then this also would put the name of Lucifer to The Sun of God. There can be no more glorious sight by definition than the rising sun, not only for its beauty and majesty but as a symbol of life, rebirth and creation and a reminder that we live another day.

Now there is a world of connotation associated in modern day with the name Lucifer thanks to hundreds of years of demonising by the 'media' Lucifer is in most religions the supposed enemy of God, however Lucifer was originally meant not as a demon, or king of the underworld but simply the fallen angel of light. And by 'media' I don't mean our modern interpretation but media as in ~ the information that is printed or reported to the masses as to the current populist world view, the world and by larger extent the universe. Media historically would include catholic and papal agenda, Kings Directives, law, word of mouth, church sermons even going as far back as the preaching of apostles.

Technology today has become the figurehead of what we understand as media, but in fact, church notices, band reading, gossip was all prior to our television, radio and newspapers and at the very heart of religious life was the church, town gatherings and the dissemination of information from the outside world all fell into the remit of the church, not just in Catholicism but all religions using synagogues and mosques alike.

Later, post Hebrew Old-Testament times, the rule of the continent and the known world was in the hands of the Romans who, as far as geography is concerned still it would seem are the centre of Catholic religious doctrine, the Vatican. And at the hands of the Romans Lucifer took his more modern name of "*Morning Star*" becoming associated more with the star that would rise in the east early in the morning just before the rising of The Sun and by doing so trumpets the arrival of *The Sun of God*, an attribute also associated with the star of the east, also known as the star of Bethlehem, which to this day is still used in Christian symbolism to denote the arrival of the *Son of God*; by putting a star on top of your Christmas tree for the twenty-fifth of December. The fairy is also used to represent the angel Gabriel who is also associated with announcing the arrival of the son of god. Further support for the pagan imagery of the Christmas tree in Europe predates Christ. The tree is a pine tree, eastern mysticism associates this with the pineal gland, the tree is traditionally daubed with baubles similar to the sephirots on the Cabbalistic tree of life and the tinsel is the snake winding around it.

Of course, we now know that this light was not actually a star, but the planet Venus and in the east is a translation from the Greek 'en te Anatole'. Which specifically describes the view of the planet Venus rising on the horizon just before dawn, at which point, as The Sun rises, the light is absorbed into that of The Sun's rays and our natural daylight.

"Aurora, watchful the reddening dawn, threw wide her crimson doors and rose filled halls; the stars took flight and in the martialled order set by Lucifer, who left his station last. Then when The Sun perceived the morning star setting and saw the world in crimson sheen and the last lingering crescent of The Moon fade in the dawn, he saw the nimble hours (Horus)." Metamorphosis – Ovid.

What made it significant for New Testament purposes is that the astronomical observers of the time were most likely not aware that Venus was not a star at all which would have a fixed observational point in the sky, but a planet that is much more transitional from our earth-centric viewpoint. Its movements would have been of great interest to the astronomers as it would not conform to the same rules as other 'stars'. And so when astronomers were awaiting the annual birth of the new sun, they observed this 'Star' briefly due to it being visible at this time of year in the area of sky during the winter solstice with Venus making its first appearance for many months at this time due to the phenomenon astrologers call 'heliacal rising'.

What follows during the next two millennia for the general population that casts Lucifer as the merged Satan and devil I believe to be a disambiguation by the Romans who already had many gods, Apollo already being named *God of The Sun*, could not possibly adapt the pseudonym of the Hebrew gods under their rule. However the morning star, rather than take equal claim to the throne of the highest upon high could appease by allowing symbioticism with other religious communities such as the Jews by simply becoming any astrological object seen as a start of the morning. In this case the planet Venus.

Lucifer was promised by God dominion over the earth subsequently however Lucifer sinned.

This was the first act ever that was not in accordance with the will of God and therefore the first sin and the creation of the concept of sin, Lucifer is the creation of sin and nominally forever more associated with sin.

We now drift off into fairy-tale. I picture a nomadic father telling his sons the story of the first ever sunrise, how God created light, which then became the first dawn and light shone on the earth for the first time in beauty and magnificent glory, reflecting off the seas and allowing people to see for the first time. What could be more beautiful than the first ever experience of sight?

And so The Sun was glorious and risen, rather than being content with being the *god of the dawn* rose above God himself and as he rose into the highest and most centre of the sky he became more beautiful than ever with its sunrays stretching out across the four corners of the world, and all the people who had until before only known darkness witnessed a new god of the skies and they worshiped and loved him like no god they had ever known before.

This pleased Lucifer and he loved their adoration such that he began to feel pride, in Isiah 14, Lucifer is described as rising above God due to pride and so it would seem the first sin created against God was pride.

God would not allow this, and so our jealous God banished him from the skies and sent him tumbling into the underworld. The fallen angel.

This is nothing more than a description of The Sun rising and setting again at the end of the day, the creation of Lucifer the morning star, ascending into heaven and then being sent back down again.

Somewhat similar to the story of Horus, Osiris and Set.

> *"How you have fallen from heaven, O star of the morning, son of the dawn! You have been cut down to the earth, you who have weakened the nations! But you said in your heart, 'I will ascend to heaven; I will raise my throne above the stars of God, and I will sit on the mount of assembly in the recesses of the north. I will ascend above the heights of the clouds; I will make myself like the Most High.' Nevertheless you will be thrust down to Sheol, to the recesses of the pit. Those who see you will gaze at you. They will ponder over you, saying, 'Is this the man who made the earth tremble, who shook kingdoms, who made the world like a wilderness and overthrew its cities, who did not allow his prisoners to go home?'" (Isaiah 14:12-18).*

As Lucifer fell he took other angels with him, these combined entities were known collectively as the Satan. Originally Satan was not a noun or figurehead personified as evil, but the collective group of fallen angels, Satan translates to 'The Adversary'.

I think visually we could be safe to assume that the angels being taken with him would be the smaller visual celestial bodies such as stars and the other planets, which from or viewpoint once The Sun had descended due to the earth's rotation, that same rotation direction, anti-clockwise would make the stars seem to follow east to west, trailing after the fallen sun.

A very good description I recently heard of Satan is 'he whom we are not' therefore Satan can be manifest only in the third person. You cannot be Satan, by that concept it would be difficult to be a fan of Satan or indeed by extension a Satanist, as if we assume that Satan is biblically the enemy or adversary to the Abrahamic religions and you became a Satanist, then by definition your Satan(adversary) would be the Christians, Muslims, and Jews (Abrahamic religions). To call yourself a Satanist in its truest form would be like referring to yourself as them. Of course, we accept that while a strong argument, Satanists have earned their claim to the use of that word to describe themselves.

'Jesus died for our sins'. And here it is, until the story of Jesus, who at Calvary defeated Satan once and for all time so God would no longer have an adversary. However each morning The Sun continues to rise. How would this tie in with the defeat of Lucifer and his league of Satan we must ask. Because in the battle, Jesus replaces Satan and thus replaces Lucifer as the *Risen Sun*. This is simply a figurehead change of a perceived battle of good and evil. The question being, which is which?

Satan is also known as the deceiver. If there is one true God and Lucifer is the rising sun or light then the one true God is logically darkness, yet we associate darkness with evil and good with light. Jesus and therefore Lucifer already have claimed to be the light; God was the creator of the light and, therefore the light is the son of God.

Putting logic aside for a short while, let us indulge in the belief that there is a celestial battle for our souls between good and evil, would not the worship of Jesus, The Sun god be the same as worshiping Lucifer. I have no doubt Jesus is Horus, Horus is Set, Set is Osiris. The one in the three, the holy trinity. However, if Jesus is Lucifer and Lucifer is the deceiver, then proclamations that you can only enter the kingdom of heaven through Jesus Christ could conceivably be a deception, his followers would theoretically worship the pretender to the throne of God; God had already declared "Thou shalt have no other gods before me" as his first and primary commandment according to Moses and Hebrew scripture yet Lucifer would not openly oppose that commandment but bend it.

What better way could there be for Lucifer to deceive all mankind than to falsify the claim of being defeated by Jesus when Lucifer is Jesus, and then claiming that you must worship 'him' to enter the kingdom of heaven. Indeed it is prophesied that during the great tribulation the army of Satan shall be cast down to earth where they will make a last futile attempt to seize control of man and the Earth (Revelations 19:20)

> ***In Thessalonians 2:1*** *Demons being the fallen angels of Satan will attempt to deceive men who will then follow Satan in a coup against God.*

The keyword being deceived as that, will mean that those men will believe they are acting in the worship of God, how else would they be classed as 'deceived'.

In early Canaanite mythology, the story is pretty much the same however the names of the gods are changed, God or the one true God was named El and the morning star that tried to overthrow him was called Hêlal. as covered in ***Exploring The Divine,*** El is the original name of God, and all things related to God Ang-El, being the mess-eng-er (Eng(Engle)) of God.

Returning to the Old Testament and my argument that it is more scientifically descriptive than commonly assumed, but written or interpreted in a very elaborate way is the opening statement of Lucifer being the 'first and most glorious creature of God' this gives us a time frame, although a very loose one.

If we return to the creation of our solar system, logically The Sun would be the first born object and king of our solar system forming from the collapse of a molecular cloud, as it remains to this day. The planets that then came later comprise the remaining objects that were also made up from the resulting gases and space dust must have first formed.

The solar-system is estimated to be approximately 4.6 billion years old, starting with The Sun, the remaining dust and gases flattening out into a disk-like shape which in turn to be later formed into our planets and moons etc. which is the current scientific thinking and apart from the way in which the mechanics of gravity works I have no dispute, this principle is known as the Nebula Hypothesis and was first proposed in the 18th century by Emanuel Swedenborg, Immanuel Kant, and Pierre-Simon Laplace.

Nobody has pinpointed the exact chronology of planetary creation, some argue that because there will resultantly be smaller objects the outer planets would have been first to form. However, that would be subjective to the question of 'at what point is a planet fully formed?'

Also, take into consideration in the early evolution of the solar system, planets may well bump together causing either smaller planets or merged larger planets depending on the circumstances of that contact.

Venus is the known as the morning star, and being The closest planet to earth is also the brightest 'star' as the ancients would perceive it in the sky, clearly we know it not to be a star but a planet, however when compared to the only other two objects in our sky that are brighter, The Sun and The Moon Venus would appear like a star with unusual behaviour in that it would not remain as static as the other stars while orbiting our sun.

This would give the illusion of being a fallen star or more poetically a fallen angel.

Other interpretation of illumination.

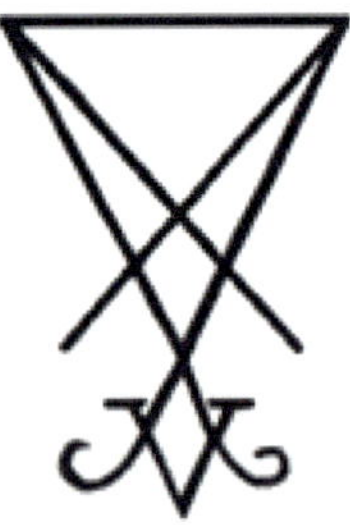

Lucifer is defined as 'the light' but in a purely spiritual sense rather than a physical one, the light would be more descriptive of a spiritual awaking. Lucifer, like all demonised angels, has a sigil (right); which closely resembles the much-maligned pentagram we see in Hollywood horror stories whose simplistic symbolism can easily associated with the devil. The sigil of Lucifer dates back to the sixteenth-century book known as the ***Grimoirium Verum***, or the 'Grimoire of Truth.' And its purpose was to bring about a visual invocation of the angel Lucifer. It is important to know that a visual invocation can be a personal experience rather than a public one. A visual manifestation is an occurrence to the observer within their mind and not necessarily a physical manifestation within our three dimensional physical plane.

In a similar fashion to an upside down crucifix the sigil of Lucifer is an inverted symbol that may not have been obvious, assuming you have ever even encountered this sigil before. Now that I have inverted it for you I hope you will see the obvious link between the sigil and that symbol which is associated with the Illuminati, ancient Egyptian symbolism that occurs even today on the US dollar bill.

Symbolism associated with the 'Them' that constitute the multitude of organisations and fraternities that from the outside world are collectively known as the Illuminati and who have symbols accredited to them, none more famous than the *all seeing eye* usually accompanied by a pyramid.

Indeed we can even draw a parallel with the symbol used by that society thought to be heavily associated with the Illuminati, the Freemasons.

Below I have overlaid the inverted symbol of Lucifer over a stone carved masonic symbol. You can see where the square aligns exactly with the square, the upper lines encircle the 'G' which supposedly represents the great architect (God) or geometry and the compass iris, sits squarely in the middle of the inverted V previously at the bottom of Lucifer's sigil creating the final symbol, the *All-Seeing Eye* once again.

Simplistic opponents to this kind of associations will conclude that such organisations are simply devil worshipers, but that is due to the culture of demonising one religious practice over another usually due to the evolution of a religion from a previous incarnation of that self-same religion which I will cover in greater detail later, or due to the diversification of one stream of religion where followers of that particular branch believe it sacrilege to worship the same divine spirit but under different hats, in such cases as the Abrahamic religions of Judaism, Christianity and Islam, who despite being effectively the same religion, fight, kill and despise one another to this day. Shame on them all.

So what does this all mean? Well Illuminati, means enlightened if you go to google ant type "what does illuminati mean" you will get this result

illuminati

/ɪˌl(j)uːmɪˈnɑːti/

noun

people claiming to possess special enlightenment or knowledge of something.
"some mysterious standard known only to the illuminati of the organization"

- a sect of 16th-century Spanish heretics who claimed special religious enlightenment.
  noun: **Illuminatus**; plural proper noun: **Illuminati**
- a Bavarian secret society founded in 1776, organized like the Freemasons.
  noun: **Illuminati**

Enlightened, is a good choice of words when referring to Luciferian '*The light bringer*' philosophy. Since Lucifer illuminates the way, he brings spiritual enlightenment in our exploration of the real.

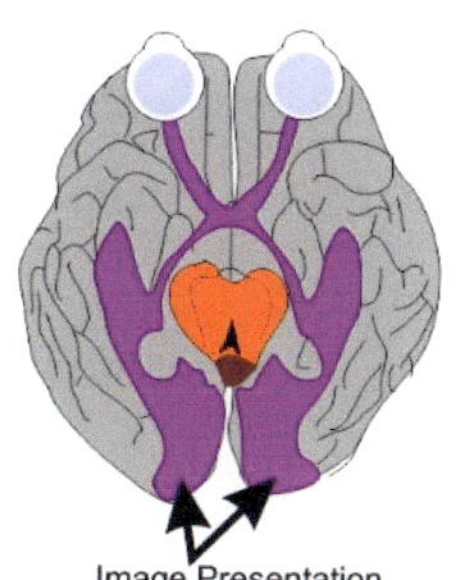

This chapter is not going to suggest that for one minute all Luciferians are members of the Illuminati nor would it suggest that all members of the of the upper echelons of the bodies of establishment that have the power to manipulate global events are either Luciferian or

Illuminati, although strong links suggest a symbiosis exists between the two.

Furthermore it should not be considered that membership of either group would indicate negative intentions towards the world or fellow man, they are both principles of betterment for mankind or the individual, and Illuminati by rumour are an elitist sect of the Luciferian philosophy.

Physicology

Most evolved earth life interacts with light through its eyes, the eye is represented heavily in many occult symbols, however it may seem strange that there is usually only one eye, yet on a physical level, logic would suggest that man should always default to two eyes being the best way for us to view things.

So why only one eye?

Well there are many reasons, we could simply suggest the all seeing eye of God being our primary deity icon (The Sun) which I think I cover throughout the book in various representations, but in the ancient tradition of the microcosm reflecting the macrocosm which is a stalwart in Kabbalistic basis and in this chapter I will relate it to the inner microcosm that in man himself.

If you speak to someone knowledgeable about our vision, or research how vision works you will be told that the part of our brain that handles what is presented to our eyes, resides right at the very back of our brain, yet despite this for many thousands of years spiritual aspects of cultures have referred to a mysterious third eye, in Hinduism this third eye is associated with the primary head chakra, the Ajna, or brow chakra.

Taoist and new age concepts undergo third eye training focusing attention on the point between the eyebrows with the purpose of aligning their spiritual 'vibration' with that of the cosmos as a part of their meditation practices.

In modern writings theosophist, H.P. Blavatsky world renowned occultist and Theosophical Society founder, associated the third eye with the pineal gland, which resides centrally between the left and right hemispheres of the brain.

The Pineal Gland

In the human brain, the Pineal gland is medically considered a relatively dormant redundant secretion gland that we have evolved to have little use for, although many reptiles including snakes use the pineal gland, not as a secretion gland but to sense light.

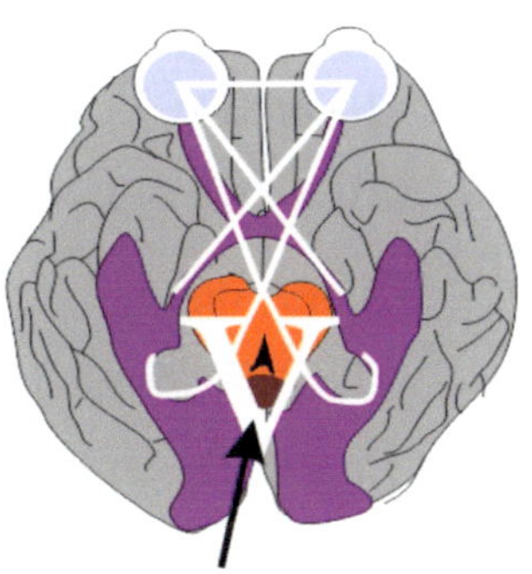

Pineal Gland

So its stands to reason that a gland used by other species to sense light but dormant for those purposes in humans may have, in man's previous incarnations along the evolutionary path, also have been a receptor of light. While we consider our faculties to have evolved for our betterment, there has clearly been a trade-off by way of losing a sense that we no longer have direct naturally occurring access to, and that is no insignificant thing. If we consider our remaining senses, or just the primary ones, such as sight, touch, hearing, taste, balance and temperature they are all essential to understanding our environment, moreover they are the foundations for that which we call 'fact'.

"Fact" ow what we consider to be facts are our subjective knowledge based on our experiences via our collective senses, but the idea that one of those senses could be missing is not easily acceptable, for example, a witness in a court of law could bring a complete change in that which is determined as an evidential occurrence. Cases in law have been lost or won by the poor eyesight of a witness, poor hearing - "How many gun shots did you hear?" And the whole case rests on the reliability of a witness to recount unhindered observations.

Facts as far as the human race is concerned, are purely defined by that which we share. A common sense of experience. Most people for example would not rely on facts presented by a spiritual medium who is claiming to have a testimony gathered by way of a conversation with the dead. This is simply because we do not share that sense that they claim to have, therefore it is not a real sense.

The knowledge that we once had a physical, provable receptor for a lost sense means that sadly we no longer have all the information that was once 'common sense'.

The question remains though, at what point of human evolution did we lose this sense? This sense would have completely changed our perception of our environment, our personal view of the universe is made up of nothing more than the cumulative input of our senses. Without whatever sense the pineal gland provided us with there is information that in our current state of evolution we cannot even perceive.

It is possible that the redundancy of the pineal gland was as recent as a few thousand years ago, evidence would suggest that our ancestors seem to be very knowledgeable on it from the times of earliest writings maybe 4,000BCE.

I would suggest that this transition may have taken place at the time when civilisation rose. Primitive man was reactionary, he lived in a world where actions gave rise to ideas. He dropped seeds of corn on his way back to his home, they got trod into the dirt and the corn grew. Man saw life, coming from death by burying things. The action of burying gave thought to the concept of rebirth.

In later stages of progression-ism ideas lead to actions, man planned and began to evolve into civilisations at this point of his evolution.

Charles Webster Leadbeater who is mentioned again later in this book when I get into the subject of *Quantum Physics* claimed that by extending an 'etheric tube' from the third eye, it is possible to develop microscopic and telescopic vision, almost a bionic eye for those who are as old as me who remember the 1970s fantasy TV show.

Most primitive religions and fables have a legend of the loss of an eye contained within their stories usually attributed to one of their personified deities, Norse legend Odin gave his eye to acquire knowledge, Horus's right eye was torn out, one of the many similar accounts of the eye of Ra, tells of Ra becoming old and weak and according to legend was being discredited by his followers and so plucked out an eye from Ureas the royal serpent that adorned his head, creating his daughter. Here we have a conjectural link between knowledge of the inner eye, its location and the relationship with reptiles. In Irish mythology Brigit in her attempts to remain a virgin (pure) plucks out one of her eyes to dissuade the attractions of the saint's brothers who claimed her eyes beautiful; could be synonymous with the loss of innocence by the loss of an eye. In Egyptian mythology the third eye as a spiritual rather than physical concept was referred to as the *Eye of Horus (also the eye of Ra),* which is represented by this hieroglyphic symbol, and strangely fitting with the diagram I showed above of how the sigil of Lucifer fits quite nicely over the top view of a cutaway to the brain like a roadmap indicating where the pineal gland

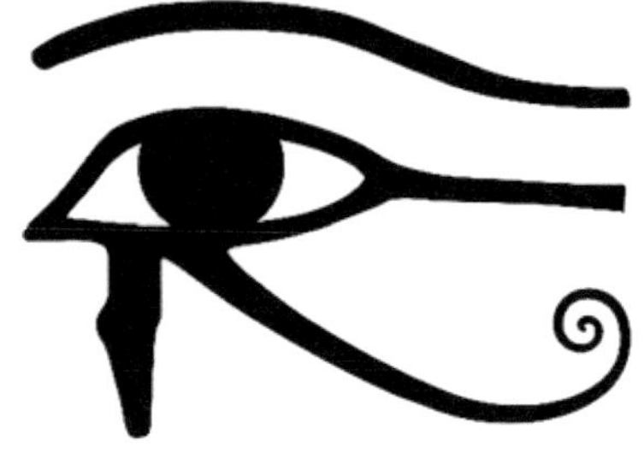

resides. If we take a side view cutaway you can see the eye of Horus icon fits very comfortably as a diagram of the pineal gland itself. This diagram is featured quite heavily on esoteric

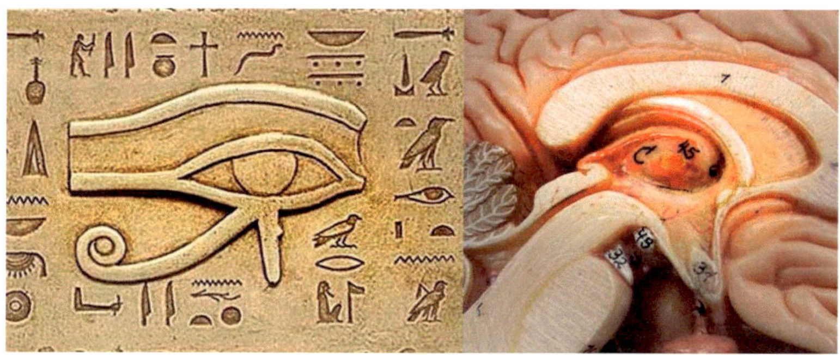

websites as an illustration of the arcane knowledge of the ancient Egyptians, I am not claiming any great revelation or credit for myself here.

Returning to biblical teachings, Mather 6:22 Jesus said

> *"The lamp of the body is the eye: if therefore thine eye be single, thy whole body shall be full of light."*

Here we have in biblical quotation a direct reference from the stories of Jesus regarding a single eye. Below we have a comparison image of Michelangelo's painting of God

reaching out and touching man, as depicted on the famous ceiling of the Sistine Chapel which was completed in 1512 A.D.

Symbolising man's divine connection to god, but what exactly is God seated in, it has been suggested that Michelangelo a known member of the Illuminati and Freemason at the time was depicting the connection to the pineal gland and divine light in the fresco.

> *1 John 1:5. This then is the message which we have heard of him, and declare unto you, **that God is light**, and in him is no darkness at all.*

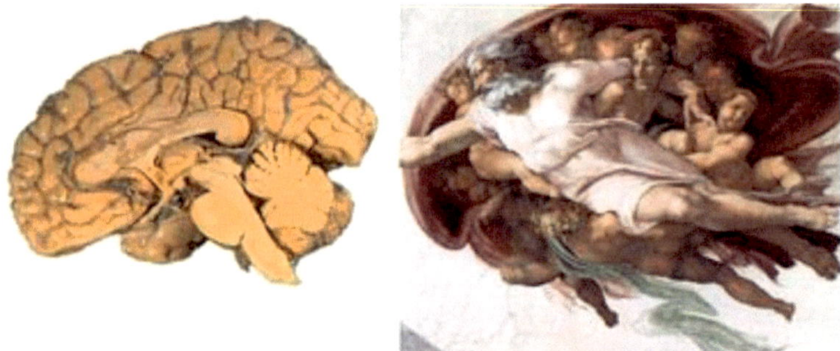

This Bible passage again emphasising that God is being of light, but it has always been taken to be a metaphor, or as I indicated in ***Exploring the Divine*** most likely a reference to God being the light of the earth and linking him to sun worship. Do we take this concept of light literally due to our loss of sensory input we attained from the pineal light? What if God, our greater unified consciousness is the light that can only be seen by the now redundant pineal gland, a sense of light contained in a photon, visible only when not viewed with the standard eye in the light frequency of radiation?

In Genesis 32:30

> *"So Jacob called the place pineal saying, "It is because I saw God face to face, and yet my life was spared."*

Luciferianism is just one of the many subsets that have diversified from the same parent group regarding spiritual connection to a greater deity, it is not witchcraft nor it is not Satanism, and it has aspects and attributes that are shared by all religions including some regarded as occult. But RHP (Right Hand Path) Luciferianism seeks to reconcile our human selves with the universal spirit that we are a part of.

The light is within us, and Gnostic RHP Luciferianism is the search to connect back to that universal consciousness. If you are Christian by upbringing you have probably been indoctrinated by your tutors that Luciferianism is devil worship so you may be surprised to find that many Luciferian's actually regard Jesus in high esteem as being a personification story of Lucifer.

Leo Taxil born 1854 was a French writer and journalist who began to associate the freemasons with Luciferianism in his exposés which mainly focused on the Catholic Church.

His attention to scorning the church seemingly diminished and redirected to free-masonry after an alleged conversion to Catholicism, after which he published a series of books and articles which decried the 'Brotherhood' in an anti-freemasonry campaign, claiming that renowned freemason Albert Pike had instructed 'The 23 Supreme Confederated Councils of the world', that Lucifer was God and he was in opposition to the catholic God. It is also true that despite masonic claims that Lucifer was the morning star in masonic ritual, they actually believed in a Satanic Lucifer.

After a period of time Taxil was able to gain audience with, and the support of the catholic church in Rome, Pope Leo XIII a former target of Taxil's vitriol endorsed his campaign by publically chastising the *Bishop of Charlston* who had previously declared some of Taxil's work to be a complete fraud, Pope Leo XIII went on to lend his blessing to an Anti-Masonic congress of Trent.

Taxil was indeed duplicitous as he gained the support of the church in his anti-masonic campaign, he later went to deliver a lecture in front of many dignitaries and members of the clergy where he thanked the church for its support but that what he had in-fact done was to expose the anti-masonic nature of the church through one of a series of hoaxes including convincing the commandant of Marseille that its harbour was shark infested, to which he sent a ship out to destroy them while another hoax included a claim that Lake Geneva actually contained an underwater city which resulted in tourists and investigators going there to see for themselves. He ended his lecture by thanking the clergy and the catholic newspapers for facilitating his greatest hoax which was his conversion which exposed the Anti-Masonic nature of the church.

This was later coined the *Taxil hoax*.

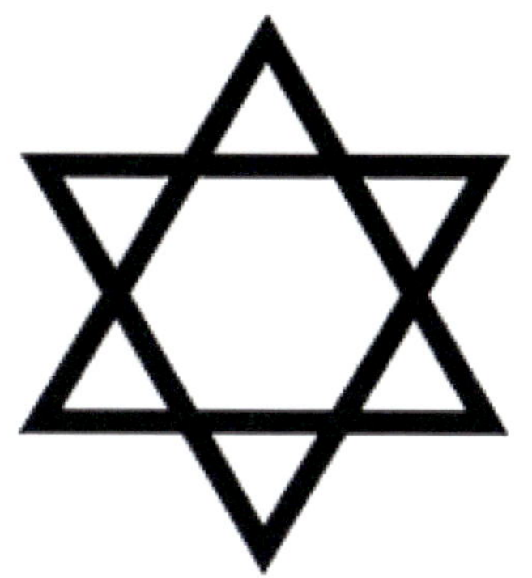

The Microcosm / Macrocosm connection is represented in many ways, textually it can be 'As above, So below' iconographically it can be two intersecting triangles such as the Hexagram a symbol shared in many cultures and faiths, Kabbalistically whatever exists in the greater cosmos that forms the body of god, also exists in the body of man and so the light bringer represented astrologically by Venus or The Sun and the combination of celestial bodies is the pineal gland in the human brain, it is our connection with god, it is through Horus, Jesus, that we can enter the kingdom of heaven, but it is lost to us, the Pineal gland, redundant and dead is in its sun set, it is blind like Höðr from Norse legend, this is evolution. But there is hope for us yet, the macrocosm is cyclic, Horus killed Set using a spear while Set was disguised or shapeshifted into the form of a Hippopotamus, we have in our brains another gland called the Hypothalamus.

The Hypothalamus

The hypothalamus is located below the thalamus, just above the brainstem and is part of the limbic system.

All vertebrate brains contain a hypothalamus. It is the key link in our nervous system and is located at the top of the spine. The hypothalamus controls body temperature, hunger, desire for earthly needs, it is the Cain to our Abel, the *Matter* to our *Aether*. And it too is a secretion gland which drives the behaviours of things like thirst, sleep, and circadian rhythms.

Secretion of two glands that for opposing spiritual and material human essences. It is maybe the physical explanation for the Norse story of Ymir.

The transition of the real (Ra-El) moving from the spiritual to the Material in man's evolution could be described as this one brother, killing another. We experience our demiurgical material world with information in the context of the physical being metamorphosed into our spiritual conscious self.

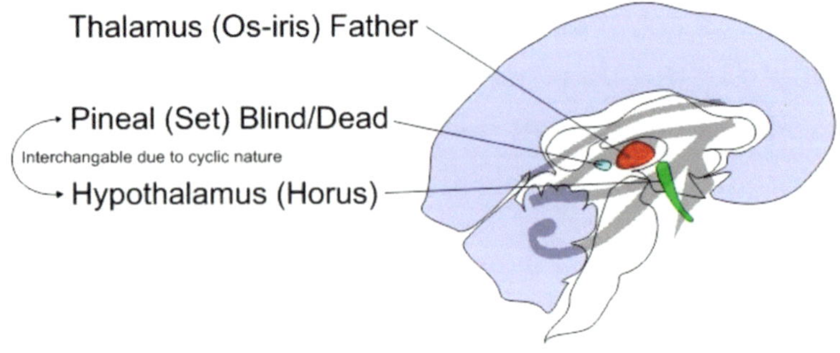

The Hypothalamus represents this metamorphosis as described astrologically and existentially in many of the described mythologies. Set disguises himself as a hippopotamus in Egyptian cycles, in the Ortherus Greek mythology is the mother figure Hippodamia raped by Eurition. Hippomania is a condition of having a passion for horses. A hippopotamus is known as a water horse.

What is pertinent to the Luciferian is the ignition of enlightenment of this gland. We are entering the age of the water bearer, Aquarius. Aquarius is Lucifer. Water bearer, is wave bearer, light is formed in waves and particles. An often omitted reference to Lu in favour of the roman light definition is the Greek where Lu (sometimes luv) is the verb to Wash, and it is where we get the word Di-Lu-te. Water like light f-lu-ds (floods), in chemistry terms associated to the microcosm of man, the excretion of chemicals (Michaels) is illumination on a personal level.

In ***Exploring the Divine*** I explained how Mi-Chai-El translates to - who life gives

Who or From (mi)

Life or Living (chia)

God or Giver (el)

It also translates similarly to the opening chapter of creation to *From Living God.*

Below is the symbol of Chai, which is often worn as a talisman of luck. Looks a bit like a horse or a cow doesn't it?

In Hebrew Chai is the lowest (closest to the physical plane) emanation of God, *"chi"* in Greek is the pronunciation of x or the cross, as in xtian a short form of the Christ. In Chi-nese Chi means 'snake', funnily enough -nese means 'serpent'. Chi is a form of energy associated with practices of Kundalini (serpent) Yoga.

The Hippocampus

Humans and other mammals have two hippocampi, one in each side of the brain, The word hippo is Greek for horse and Kampos means Sea-Monster, This is the water bearer side of the light-bearer Hypothalamus.

The Hippocampus gets its name due to its resemblance to a Sea-Horse (See picture right). It is another component of the *Limbic system* and is responsible for modelling our memories into their long term and short term attributes, it distinguishes what our subjective mode of current observation is and our long term subjective mode by accumulated knowledge. Hippocampus is Horus.

The Hippocampus is also responsible for our special awareness, located under the cerebral cortex (Guarded by Cerberus)

How could Greeks, Ancient Egyptians, or even earlier Sumerian or any historic legend of mankind's makeup possibly have been this knowledgeable on matters of brain surgery that we can only now begin to guess at, the ability to scan live brain functions, simply a hack handed cut out of these parts of the brain to see what they do isn't conceivable.

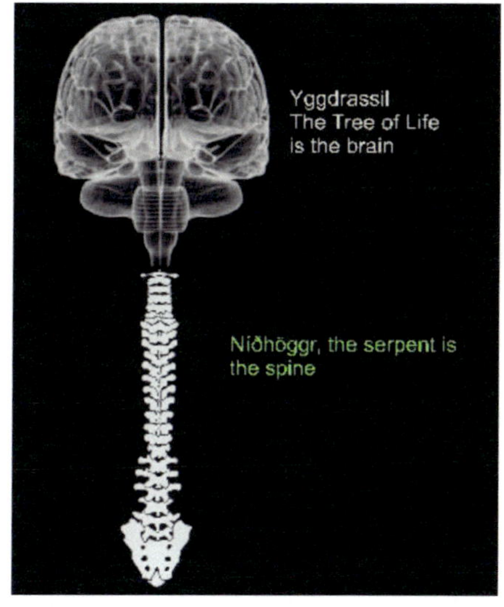

The *Age of Lucifer* is now and will be for the next 2,200 years. The cosmic awaking is reflected in the microcosm of the human condition.

The dawn is upon us, and like the hippo's eyes appearing above the water, like a sunrise out of the horizon, we as a race are awakening to a new future. The early orange effects of the dawn are here and the old Piscean religion is being cast aside, the fall of Catholicism which corrupted Christianity's good nature into a profit seeking manipulation and moral slavery of man is all but dead.

Ave Lucifer.

Lucifer is not evil, Lucifer has been portrayed as evil, and it is the true light, the life, The Sun of Man.

The eternal torment of being God

Once you adopt the mind-set of the infinite nature of everything and realise that everything must exist in a boundless universe, you must quantify it by reasoning that also nothing exists with predetermined absolute, our concept of the universe is merely an interpretation of our senses and experience primarily subjective and then influenced by collective agreement.

The infinite nature of everything insists that all things are collectively one thing, the universe, comprised of its internal components, much like a car is a combination of components known collectively as a car.

The ultimate power of the universe and its collective consciousness is made up of all the individual consciousness's whom may not be aware of the greater collective consciousness, these individuals comprise the collective God, who before dispersal and upon being self-aware created the universe, either intentionally or as a result of its own insanity.

You see, we create our subjective reality. We create our version of reality based up the experiences we perceive; all realities are purely observational to the individual and his ability to manipulate it.

The next question is "How can so many individuals create their own existence that doesn't fly in the face of others versions of existence?" This paradox creates a need for a universal law, a law that governs a shared experience of reality, it stands to reason that if we created those experiences on a subconscious level, we also created multiple versions that exist independent of each other as observed by others. The combination of these two levels of consciousness creates the content of the artificial universe we live in.

The universal law is merely an act that dictates that certain information is not available for manipulation to individual consciousness' and is dictated by a higher level consciousness that inhibits information being passed between these units.

Our individual view of that higher level consciousness as perceived from this side of the fence can for want of a better term be called God, although collectively the two hemispheres of the entity is what really makes the whole.

This combination of the higher and lower consciousness would be the *'All Knowing God'*. The higher consciousness could, therefore, be referred to as the Father, and we it's individual offspring the sons (or daughters, this is just a metaphor and nothing to do with sex in this instance).

Between the overseeing father and the individual consciousness of ourselves, the sons, we would make the third distinctive entity that of the 'All Knowing God' and between the three distinct areas of the whole create the universal Holy Trinity.

For example if we consider one of our experiences, an individual memory within the brain, perhaps your first childhood memory of playing on a swing, that memory although a form of its own consciousness is not aware of other memories that also exist within the very same brain. Those recordings for want of a better word are recollected data streams that usually have a fixed beginning, middle and end are contributory factors in our perception of the world. We, much like the overseer God hemisphere are the masters of recalling those entities as individual portions of reality; collectively they make us the whole.

We can combine that recollection into a cumulative experience we call our childhood, we can also if we wish manipulate those memories to create a new version of our experienced reality, and since those particular segments of memory are unique to us from our observant perspective we effectively can change subjective history.

Your only obstacle on doing so would possibly be the memory of another individual and their version of events. This is where the universal law of observation kicks in. However, this does not make it impossible to change these events it simply makes it more difficult.

Like those memory streams, we as humans and as a part of the ultimate consciousness that is God, are not aware of other consciousness unless we experience events within the shared experience according to the universal law of observation.

Our sentience is limited to this, our specific area of gods mind.

The whole universe is an illusion created by the great consciousness who then created the universal laws of observation so that the individual consciousness may experience existence with boundaries as being self-aware and nothing else, for eternity, would be insufferable damnation if we remained a solipsistic entity.

Once we truly realise that we generate our own existence, lifespan, even death we gain knowledge of 'the truth'. Since mankind can recall we spoke of 'the truth' as being the word of God, and what that truth is, is fairly inconceivable, we have hidden it from ourselves as God.

The truth is we are alone. Not as a species on a planetary level but, in essence, there is no individual me, no individual you, no collective we, only I, I AM.

So if you were the sole single entity in existence it would be a devastating concept to exist with. Imagine for a second the solipsistic view that you are God, and the only entity in existence, nothing and no one else exists, just you, in the void for all eternity. But you are not even substantial. You are consciousness alone.

You have all power over existence. But nothing exists, you have to create existence from the imagination, yet you know that it is still a lonely sad existence. You could create an existence in your imagination or even other people somewhat like a child's imaginary friend, you have that power and I'm sure this was a part of the process. However, it would quickly be abolished as you would be aware that they were figments of your imagination and even with their own consciousness would be aware that they were fictitious.

So the next option would be to make the consciousness unaware of each other with dominion only over their own sphere of individualism.

These would be the polytheist gods of old, the first beings, and their dominions would be very radical things in the universe, we at this stage wouldn't have the intricate and complex universe we see today, it would be a very basic one of just a few simple but highly diverse elements, aware that collectively they made the whole, but individually unaware of their counterpart's consciousness, this would allow God to explore new avenues of existence in the form of company with an unknown quantity and without a predetermined outcome.

The process of what happened next would have two possibilities, either there was conflict over dominance of existence which resulted in one god eliminating all others creating the whole and then the realisation repeats itself, or there was a collective decision to create a division between the higher levels of consciousness and the lower levels creating a hierarchy structure.

This hierarchy structure would ensure that there was always a higher level consciousness being aware of all things, right at the top of the pile, he would then for the sake of sanity, create a law that meant no other consciousness would have such oversight, and he alone would suffer the insufferable loneliness of knowing he was the one.

He could not make his presence known to the lower entities as this would lead to their self-realisation of being imagined from the single entity.

They too being some of the original gods would repeat this, taking the hierarchy down to the lowest form of consciousness, the individual memories in our brain that has no awareness of other memories however collectively we gain information from them which shapes our existence.

The triangular hierarchy this represents has been depicted many times in belief systems trying to alert us to its place in the universe. It could be a simplistic chart drawing God at the top, seraphim as the next level, angels and the next man as the next or in the form of dominion of those components such as the elements Air, Fire, Water and Earth.

The state of none existence,
a point before time, and matter, a state of nothingness
nothingness cannot exist without an opposite so
something must have existed within the void.

This would be the conciseness that we can only refer to as God, the unity of all things without physical attributes existing before time and after time. infinite.

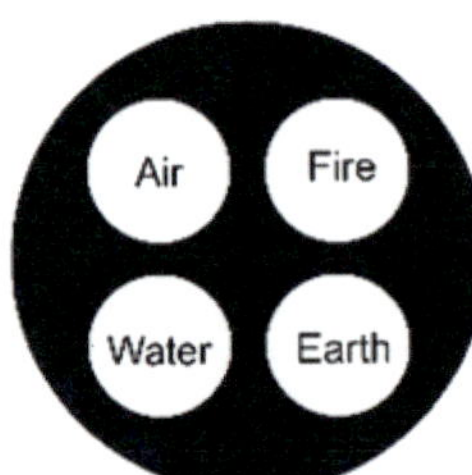

God would divide himself into the elements giving rise to the multiple gods, these would either be entities who are aware they are a part of god and therefore still suffer the lowliness or be forced to believe they are independent entities which would create sanity, but also rivalry or domination

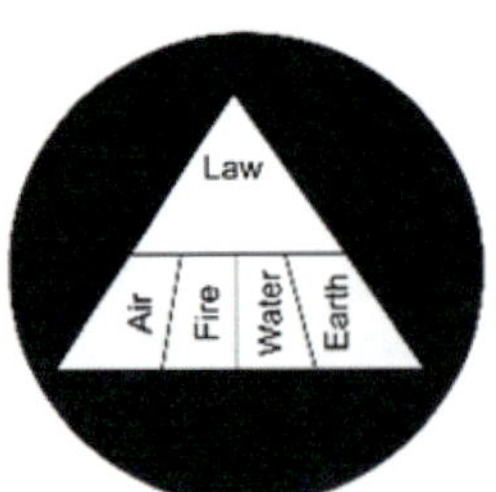

Law would sacrifice its self to the entities of the universe so that they will not know their true state of being the omnipotent, it would make the law which maintains balance in the universe by becoming overseer but must appear to remain intangible to itself, this allows its other selves to believe in a greater self rather than the only self.

It is entirely possible that man created lasting monuments to this structure intent to survive millennia.

Chichen Itza, Mexico (2014)

The photograph above represents just such a legend. It is Chichen Itza in Mexico where there is a three dimensional lasting iconograph of such a structure, with a single overseeing master on top and the four elements or seraphim of creation descending, likewise it is believed that the pyramids at Giza had a cap made of pure gold.

Ancient structures provide a lasting representation of the blueprint for the conscious creation of the universe as handed down to us.

The very structure of a pyramid has a greater significance to the embodiment of mortality than you would at first give it credit for. Unlike an obelisk or great tower there is a significance to the narrow top compared to the wide and intrusive bottom, in an hermetic sense the material

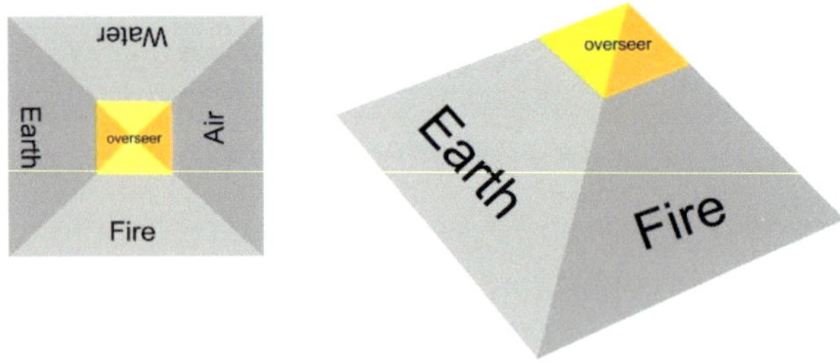

components are earthly and spiritual components such as air or the aether are exalted, to be on high. The triangle shape represents the upward progression from man's demiurgical form in the gnostic sense to his higher spiritual nature, without weight or measure and god-like, the divine self.

The similarities in structures and symbology between the Incas/Aztecs and The Egyptian is obvious and undeniable, yet there is no evidence that these two cultures on opposing sides of the planet had any contact with each other whatsoever, yet we must draw the conclusion that their sources for this body of work in their buildings and sculptures, arts or reliefs are inspired from the same source. In fact both cultures built stepped stone pyramids, mummified the revered of the dead which were then interned in the pyramids themselves crossing the arms of the dead in the same way we do even today. Their gods were often featured in reliefs that depicted their gods holding staffs made of snakes who were sun worshipers, in fact almost every aspect of the two cultures are duplicated.

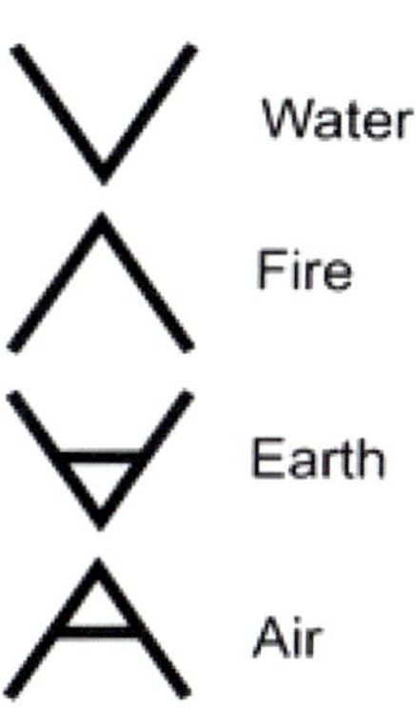

When elemental symbols are represented in two dimensional illustrations you will notice that the elements of air and earth still retain the cap, is this more than just to distinguish them from fire and water, or is it telling us that God no longer has dominion over the elements? If as a collective consciousness our consciousness is truly a part of god's collective consciousness, could this be indicating that man no longer has dominion over fire and water, and maybe we did once. Yes we can manipulate it, but we breathe air and have evolved to live on the land, however we cannot exist in either fire or water, and earth can be considered as matter when you categorise the universe into these four base elements as the ancients believed.

In fact, the four basic elements were in good stead until very recently in the course of human development. Obviously today we have a much wider understanding of the makeup of things in the universe, however the four principle elements can still be divided into liquids, gases, solids and fire which I believe is best represented by the consumption or turning into energy of any of these three simplistic elements.

Even great thinkers such as Leonardo Da Vinci were firmly believed in the four element approach to nature and the universe.

Lucifer, Satan and the Serpent

You may be wondering why I would include Satan in a book that is Luciferian oriented, well it is due to the nature of this book not being a guide on how to be, or practice Luciferianism, more an anthropology of its origin, development and with hints of Luciferian philosophy, for these purposes, as you will have seen already there is a lot of crossover between names and legend or mythology in all mythological characters, Satan and Lucifer similarly are subject to that.

That does not in any way infer that the philosophies of Satanists and Luciferians are the same, while similarities exist in the legendary characters, the outlooks and goals have very clear divisions, Luciferians do not distinguish between good and evil, Luciferians acknowledge the balance between the two and are neutral in their perspective of it, their actions are not usually in any way considered evil, they act either for self-gratification or betterment of something they believe in. I know of no section of Luciferian ideology that aims to destroy or cause harm intentionally to anyone else, that's not to say that they would not be ruthless in their pursuit of their goal.

You should look at it as though it is a major corporation whose takeover of another company may cause redundancies that are considered collateral damage to the growth of the parent company.

Satanists in the simplest definition believe in a hierarchy and deities, they primarily are anti-christian but much like Luciferian they are a broad and complex society with many concepts specific to individuals, so my apologies to any Satanist who may object to my simplistic explanation, however I defend myself by stating that this book is awash with the complexities of Lucifer and that you would need your own book on Satan rather than me trying to fit your pantheon of concepts into this one. For the whole, a Luciferian does not worship Lucifer, a Satanist might and he might consider Lucifer to be one of the many names of Satan, to the Luciferian, Lucifer is the medium for enlightenment or purely iconographic of the philosophy itself, not the object of it. However that said, in mythological context the Lucifer character gets embroidered into Satan myth.

Satan is a Christian/Judaism creation that describes the pagan gods and those that preceded the contemporary god of the Abrahamic faith. As set by the precision of the equinox (details of this can be found in the next chapter). As such, all gods that are not Abrahamic/Christian gods are Satan (The Enemy or The Adversary), so this would include Lucifer, but not make Luciferians Satanists outside of this obscure reference.

The snake has always been one of if not the strongest re-occurring symbol in religious iconography, all the way from the *Garden of Eden* to modern day mysticisms. So the concept of the snake cannot be simplified into a quick definition of what it means in historical beliefs, firstly I apologise for the overly long and complex rationale that I must get through before I actually get to the interesting stuff about the snake.

It is commonly assumed that in the *Garden of Eden* the snake represents Satan, however Satan at the time of that writing was never the *Horned God* such as we depict him now, our modern day concept of Satan as a nominal character is an amalgamation of the pagan 'horned one' which was a late comer in mythology, and not one and the same as intended to be represented in both 'geographic region' and for 'the time period' associated with the writing of the Old Testament. Although again due to the precession of the equinox, the predecessors of the *Age of Pisces,* which we are currently reaching the end of were preceded by Aries and Taurus, who both have horns so the iconic Satan would probably have horns.

In that time as said, Satan was simply the enemy or adversary of the current teaching of spiritual faith, therefore Satan would be any principle or doctrine contrary to absolute and contemporary religious faith such as alternate faiths including science or politics, scientific observations that may have even predated the Old Testaments radical new ideas.

We have a similar notion going on even now in our enlightened times where the doctrine of the establishment enforce a version of events so vigorously that it becomes difficult to apply an overruling logic.

It would be nice to think at the time when the word Satan began losing its specific meaning to becoming a generic term for bad or evil that the contemporaries of that transition would put their foot down and stop it from creating a millennium of confusion, but here we are again, even today allowing our governments to repeat the mistakes of our ancestors.

The snake in the *Garden of Eden,* is often referred to as a representation of Satan and Satan itself represents many things, and one of those things is the status quo of science that was established before the current doctrine of the Old Testament. This would bring about the creation of the word 'Philistine'.

The word Philistine is again a corruption of a definition such as described above, we often refer to a person who seems to object to the concept of something that is already regarded as an established belief by telling them they are a philistine because it's dictionary definition is 'a person who is hostile or indifferent to culture and the arts.'

The history behind the word is biblical of nature as the Philistine people were believers in an older faith, the faith that was prior to that of the more modern Hebrew teachings such as the Old Testament, the word itself even now is contemporary as these people lived in area we now call Palestine, and we still to this day have conflict there between the people of Israel (Hebrew) and the People of Palestine (Islam).

Ironically in ***Exploring the Divine*** I stated that religion did not cause any wars, more that it was the corruption of man who sought political, geographical and financial gain calling for the support of one faith as to identify the people of an alternate faith as the enemy, 'devil worshipers', 'Satanists 'to validate their case for war. Seems we have learned nothing and we continue to use faith to create divisions in people who for the whole, just want to have peace.

The Philistines are the descendants of the biblical character Mizraim who in turn was a descendant of Ham, son of Noah and brother to Shem and it is thought that they originated from the Greek island of Crete from where they migrated to the area known today as Gaza, so logic dictates if you want to start looking for Noah's Ark then Crete would be a good place to start, the Hebrews, however, are the descendants of the biblical character Jacob some generations later who is also known by the name of Israel, Jacob had a son called Judah and this gives us our modern day Jews (descendants of Judah) and going back even more generations the people of Shem (sematic), although there are several generations between the sematic tribes to those of Judah, I just thought I would throw that in there for your information.

You can perceive this modern conflict as an age-old battle between two Middle Eastern tribes or as a family quarrel. How sad it is today that this battle probably started 4,000-8,000 years ago over two probably nomadic tribes and were the cause of such upheaval in modern times.

In the book of Numbers: 21

> *"And the people spake against God, and against Moses, Wherefore have ye brought us up out of Egypt to die in the wilderness? for there is no bread, neither is there any water; and our soul loatheth this light bread.*
>
> *And the Lord sent fiery serpents among the people, and they bit the people; and much people of Israel died.*
>
> *Therefore the people came to Moses, and said, We have sinned, for we have spoken against the Lord, and against thee; pray unto the Lord, that he take away the serpents from us. And Moses prayed for the people.*
>
> *And the Lord said unto Moses, Make thee a fiery serpent, and set it upon a pole: and it shall come to pass,*

> *that every one that is bitten, when he looketh upon it, shall live."*

I find the interesting part of that description is the word 'Fiery'. We can imagine the people of Moses crossing the desert, and when they started getting dissatisfied with Moses' leadership starting to bellyache and so God would send snakes to punish them, but how would you imagine a snake as being fiery?

Could this be a reference to a meteor storm? That would be most obvious, but then it says many Israelites died, and that is highly unlikely. Then what is this fiery serpent set upon a pole?

Moses made this pole and out of Brass he placed atop the fiery snake symbol that even today is used to represent medicine, the symbol comprises of two entwined snakes with angelic wings above. It was said that anyone who gazed upon the staff while they were suffering the poison by the snakes would be cured, so we have established that the snakes bit the Israelis rather than burned them.

Snakes are a symbol of life, and death, rebirth by the way they shed their skin, their venom can bring death and was one of the very first medicines and was used to induce hallucinogenic states for shamanistic practices.

On the picture (right) you can see the symbol used in medicine today, it is known as the Caduceus although it is claimed that this is incorrect when used in association with Greek mythology. In Roman and Greek mythology it was carried by Hermes and Mercury and was referred to as the swelling on the rod of caduceus, which again gets more coverage later in the book. In Greek mythology a similar single snake coiled around a rod is used to denote health, this is the rod of Asclepius.

The rod or staff of Asclepius comes from the legend of the Greek god of the same name who presided over medicine and has temples in Epidaurus and Kos, another one of the Greek Islands establishing links between Greek mythological families and Old Testament families such as Noah and Moses.

Interestingly, particularly to my fellow countrymen the Hebrew word for snake is Nahash whose root is NHS. For the wider audience this is the symbolic name for our free healthcare system which is the mainstay of all medical related matters in the United Kingdom founded in 1948 and stands for National Health Service.

In Aztec culture, a snake with two heads was also important to their beliefs as artefacts created in this period often feature the two headed or entwined snakes that were commonly worn by tribe leaders or decision makers.

In *The Book of the Dead* an ancient Egyptian text relating to the principles of death and funerary practices written approximately 1550bc which remained as part of ceremonial practices and beliefs in the area right up until approximately 50bc there is a section entitled '*Making the transformation in to the serpent Sata*'

It clearly does not take much of a leap for us to envisage the link between the nominal title Sata and that of our modern day Sata'n.

In hermetic texts, staffs or staves have a habit of being turned into snakes, this I feel presents much imagery in a wide range of concepts, it is the rigid becoming pliable, the line becoming the curve which leads into Pythagorean principles.

The Chancellor-in –Chief,nu, triumphant saith:-

> *"I am the serpent Sata whose years are many. I die and am born again each day. I am the serpent Sata which dwelleth in the uttermost parts of the earth. I die, and I am born again, and I renew myself, I grow young each day."*

This in many ways holds great similarities to modern Christian worship and funerary prayers specifically when focusing on the resurrection of life. To die and to be born anew.

The description of the daily rebirth of this entity can be attributed to either a resurrection belief, post mortem of a person, but also greatly reflects The Sun worship principle. A daily rebirth of something dwelling in the uttermost parts of the earth from a visual perspective would be the rising from the ground, that of The Sun.

When you tie in the timeline of the demise of this sun worship funerary ritual to 50bc a clear link emerges to the change of belief from that Solarian system to the Christian era. Christian beliefs were, therefore, revolutionary but incrementally so. The change in worship is both categorical but subtle. The old ways were now frowned upon, yet the method of worship was adopted, almost like a franchise brand name change.

Scientifically speaking, or rather scientifically questioning is this correlation between the rebirth of The Sun daily and our personal human beliefs in reincarnation after death into a new life either physically or spiritually which is universally shared by every faith and therefore the answer to the unified theory of everything?

Is the reason we bury people underground simply mimicking the early belief that The Sun disappeared underground and, therefore, to be reborn again we too must reproduce the ceremony with our departed?

I suspect it is, what I wonder is, is there any fabric to this, the ancients beliefs although open to interpretation seem to me to have foundation in what we still see in modern day science where philosophical principles of the likes of Plato and Aristotle still hold water in matters of ethics, mathematics and logic can perhaps also hold true for the integration of physics to religion.

So at the birth of Christianity, Sata the old God, became a persona non grata therefore making both Serpents and Satan the enemy once again.

In the principle that *Sata the Serpent* is The Sun then how do we equate the linear shape of a snake to that of the spherical shape of The Sun? Well that's quite simple, returning to the observational perspective of sun observers, who despite popular belief, already were aware of the spherical nature of the earth were basing their principle on an earth-centric viewpoint, the head of the snake being the current location of The Sun, and his eternal path forming the circular tail of the snake.

I refer here to a diagram from my previous book, ***Exploring the Divine***, the picture of Ouroboros. Symbolic of life, death and rebirth.

So far in that premise, the only flawed logic our ancestors seemed to have on this subject which has now been debunked is the principle of the orbit of The Sun around the earth, however as Luciferians we objectively view the universe subjectively, therefore our sun from our perspective does indeed rotate around our earth if only when we consider ourselves the focal point of our universe, we care little for the collective view dictated by others.

At this point we return to the Moses story that started this chapter. And my interest in the fiery serpent.

> *"And the Lord said unto Moses, Make thee a fiery serpent, and set it upon a pole: and it shall come to pass, that every one that is bitten, when he looketh upon it, shall live."*

Breaking down the attributes of this statement we have a 'fiery serpent' which we have now theorised is Ouroboros or The Sun. 'Set upon a pole' would kind of throw my analogy a bit, in relation to The Sun. But bear with me, "and it shall come to pass", I believe is not a prophecy but a misinterpreted description of the passage of time and that all that shall see it, shall live.

I now introduce you to a quite modern interpretation of our planetary spiral as diagrammed by *'Planetary Spiral Motions and Miller's Ether-Drift.'*

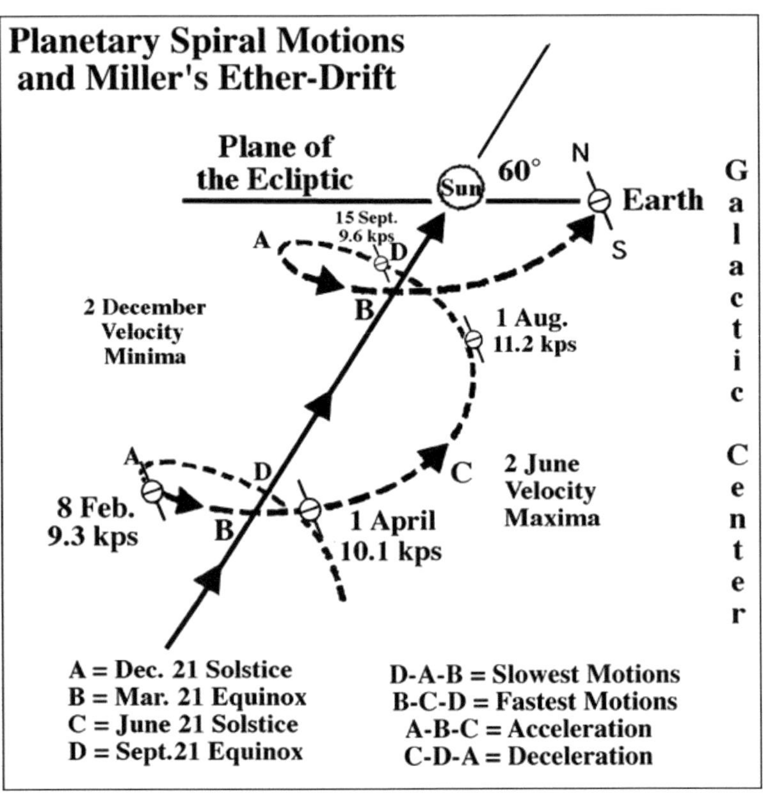

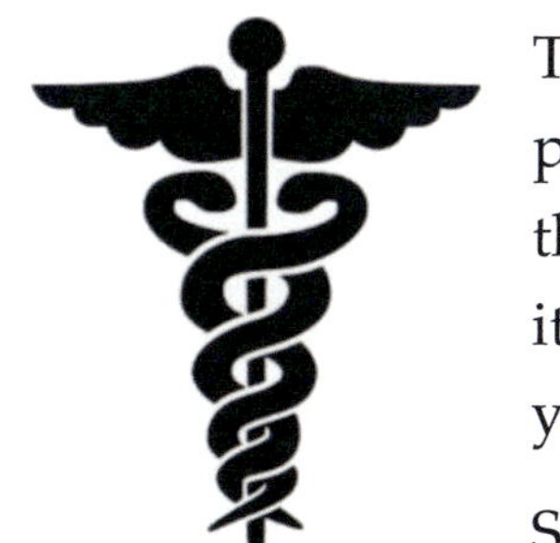

The central diagonal bar is clearly the passage of time, with The Sun at the top of this pole and a second object (the earth) and its spiral orbit of The Sun throughout the year.

So we have two snakes, representing orbits. The current position being denoted by the snakes head, entwined and related, but passing through time together in parallel. Give it wings to represent flight through the Aether and what do we get if redrawn in iconography, that will make you live.

In 1907 a liberal catholic bishop and prominent occultist by the name of Charles Webster Leadbeater wrote an article entitled 'Killion – The Aether of Space' describing the components of the atom, this was at the same time as the world's greatest physicists such as Max Planck, Niels Bohr, Lummer and Wien were revolutionizing the standard theory with the new model we know today as quantum physics.

His building blocks of the atom were described as the structure of physical matter and they were described as a spiral structure which again spirals around yet another spiral, strung on a loop in fractal coils, which was represented by this drawing. An almost identical icon to that of the planetary rotation spiral reproduced on a microscopic level.

Leadbeater describes the diagram as:-

> *"To help us to understand more clearly let us examine the ultimate atom of the physical plane. (See Figs. 3 and 6.) It is composed of ten rings or wires, which lie side by side, but never touch one another. If one of these wires be taken away from the atom, and as it were untwisted from its peculiar spiral shape and laid out on a flat surface, it will be seen that it is a complete circle--a tightly twisted endless coil. This coil is itself a spiral containing 1,680 turns; it can be unwound. And it will then make a much larger circle. There are in each wire seven sets of such coils or spirillae, each finer than the preceding coil to which its axis lies at right angles. The process of unwinding them in succession may be continued until we have nothing but an enormous circle of the tiniest imaginable dots lying like pearls upon an invisible string. These dots are so inconceivably small that many millions of them are needed to make one ultimate physical atom. They appear to be the basis of all matter of which we at present know anything; astral. mental and buddhic atoms also are built of them, so we may regard them as the fundamental units of which all material atoms on any plane yet attainable are composed.*

These units are all alike, spherical and absolutely simple in construction. Though they are the basis of all matter, they are not themselves matter; they are not blocks but bubbles. They do not resemble bubbles floating in the air, which consist of a thin film of water separating the air within them from the air outside, so that the film has both an outer and an inner surface. Their analogy is rather with the bubbles that we see rising in water, bubbles which may be said to have only one surface--that of the water which is pushed back by the confined air. Just as the bubbles are not water, but are precisely the spots from which water is absent, so these units are not koilon but the absence of koilon--the only spots where it is not--specks of nothingness floating in it, so to speak, for the interior of these space-bubbles is an absolute void to the highest power of vision that we can turn upon them."

It is easy to see how the snake occurs frequently across many cultures, especially in reference to life and the creation of, fertility often associated with the woman's role in the creation of life also needs a man's input. The snake is often used to represent this component. With the additional feature of a real snake shedding its skin, this is can be used to represent rebirth. The Serpent known as Kundalini was said to be coiled at the bottom of the spine to the unenlightened soul.

And in the Adam and Eve myth the serpent that brought knowledge and therefore enlightened man by offering the knowledge symbolised by the apple to Eve is both Lucifer and Kundalini.

In Sumerian beliefs the serpent entity is known as Enki who is paired with a brother Enlil (Lilith?), again this story is repeated, in almost every early story of the creation of mankind enlightenment or knowledge, self-awareness was given to man by the serpent like creature.

Hinduism the serpent called Shesha-naga or Ananta (satan?) which means the eternal celestial snake which Lord Vishnu rests upon, is symbolic of limitless power. A similarly written Buddhist word is anattā (Pali) which refers to the perception of 'not-self,' classically The Adversary or Satan is defined as 'That which we are not'. The enemy is not always the evil one, he is principally just an enemy. In duality an opposition is essential to existence in Yin/Yang diametric opposition to create the whole.

Pre-Ice age Civilisation

Earlier I discussed the thought that man's real period of civilisation began in Mesopotamia around 4,000 BCE as resultant settlers embarked on a period of development from the end of the Ice Age which occurred at around 9,000 BC.

The end of the ice age provided a period of resettlement as the ice glaciers melted and receded from their outreaches as far south as North Africa. All that possibly remains is the artic regions where it currently resides in the north and south poles which retain their cold. It is thought that these areas retain this low temperature due to being distant from The Sun by half the earth's diameter permanently, and The Sun being low on the horizon. This makes little sense to me, as this dictates that the earth not only sits in the 'goldilocks zone' of our solar system, but the exact centre of it, and since all of our earth spends at least half its time outside of any sunlight, if the temperatures were that drastically different then we would freeze every night, as we would be twice as far away in the equator. Just a thought.-

To keep us on track with the astrological ages it is important to know when man makes his leaps of advancement, 6,500 B.C. to *3,700 B.C. was approximately the occurrence of the age of Gemini and 8,700B.C. to 6,500 B.C. would be the age of Cancer so would have been the age directly following the Ice Age, another pivotal moment for the change in mankind's evolution both in terms of religious ideology and way of life as a whole.

The last ice ages came and went over a period of around two million years, let's get that into perspective? Man has developed from spear-wielding tribesmen to where we are today in less than ten thousand years, prior to that he was essentially a caveman and the primitive mind is described as superstitious, childlike and incapable of either critical or sustained thought. The man of Northern Europe stood on snow drifts and glacial waves over a mile deep, as the ice age covered the entire northern hemisphere with hard ice.

For two million years the northern hemisphere man had little or no access to solid land for any period long enough to establish a fixed root civilisation, unable to build structures due to lack of materials and solid foundations, he walked on mile high snow, during the intermittent global warm ups which lasted maybe a thousand years at a time, approximately twenty generations of man would have to adapt to the new environment only to have it lost again. This would preclude him from having the physical capability to develop the agriculture or architecture we credit the Mesopotamians with. Even if he had the technological ability, and if he did? Surely during these relief periods, all evidence would be destroyed by the enormity of the corrosive power of an age of ice.

Hominid man has existed for seven million years, only the past two million years has he been what we can relate to as being near as damn it, our current version of the human being and then further to that only for the past 4,000 years do we have any form of documents describing the acquired knowledge of man throughout our entire history.

And let's suggest the theory that prior to the period accredited to the Mesopotamians culture, the ice age, man did have a great deal of civilisation ability but it repeatedly became annulled by the destruction caused by the ice age, any building not megalithic in structure would be completely obliterated by such forces. I know that is contrary to what we have been taught in schools or rather since we had schools, which is a very recent development on the grand scale of things.

Also consider the lifespan of knowledge, how long would that knowledge last while not required, could you make an igloo? No doubt during the ice age only 11,000 years ago, igloo building would probably be a standard skill even for a ten-year-old, we've seen pictures of Igloo's and thanks to TV and books we probably could make one, but without the TV and books, in the same situation, we probably would resort to caves and holes in the snow.

In other words the skills would quickly be forgotten, you only have to go to an antique shop and I'm sure you'll find some tool or device and not have a clue what it was used for. Unless you have a reason to, such as being involved in that particular trade or you are an antique dealer.

Not only skills, but social dynamics would change between settlers and those still nomadic and isolation would bring about the diversity of language, social hierarchy, customs and beliefs.

Astrology

I will quickly cover the basic astrology I have been implying throughout the book so far, simply to recap on the relationships to the heavenly bodies which are macrocosmic elements of the physiological human elements such as the Hippocampus mentioned earlier.

Venus

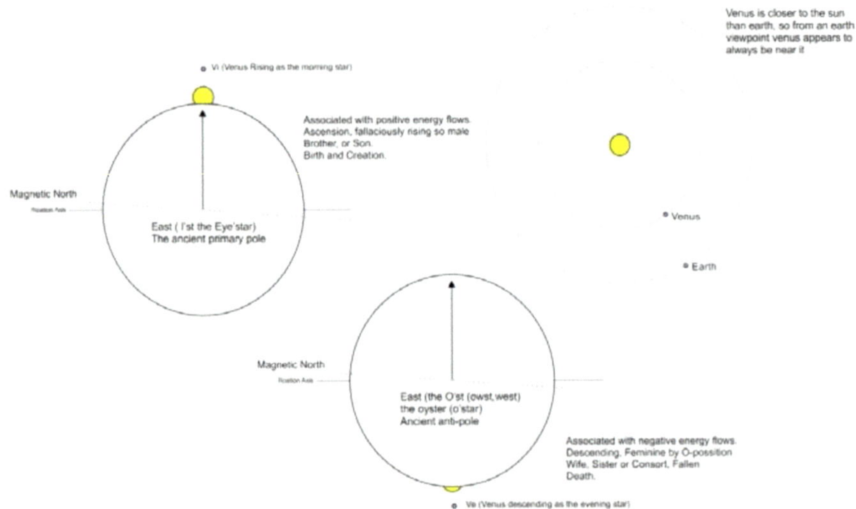

The morning star is Venus, all pantheons religions and mythos as far as I am concerned are hidden symbolic stories of Venus, a proclaimer to the throne of Sol, Helios, our Sun. which due to the fact that it is closer to The Sun in its orbit than we are, but not as close as mercury which to the human eye is obfuscated at all times, it seems too precede or follow The Sun around our heavens, sometimes it rises in the morning before The Sun, claiming the throne, ascending above the true god of our heavens, it takes pride and mastery of the sky and all the others stars as angels, then it is killed or obliterated when the true Sun and god of our heavens rises by the pure brilliance of its light, taking all other stars with it. By the time the evening comes, it may follow The Sun into the underworld or hell, possibly it can be viewed as descending to earth as one of the many fallen angels who sought to overthrow God.

Astrologers recorded these events, being planets (wanderers in Greek) as they travelled through the year and the astrological years between the fixed stars that form our distant universe, each given names based on their shapes, different cultures gave these constellations different names, The Milky Way, the lactating cow or holy mother, Virgo the virgin mother, who begins the year and ends the year, the *womb to the tomb* figure. The brothers, Ve and Vi, Cain and Abel, are faces of the dog, sometimes brother and sister, other times man and wife.

The story of betrayal, murder, rape, and renewal, the brother taking the kings throne, only to lose it again.

The snake, the bull and the horse, cycle, duality and desiring the attention of the father.

Although I have stolen some of the divine belief and placed all these stories into a mechanical and scientific context, I am still a theist. We have to ask ourselves why this one story has travelled the earth with different characters. What is the story trying to tell us? I know and have repeated the Macrocosm equals the microcosm, man is created in Gods image, God is the whole body of the universe and we are a physical component in that body, we are God and God is speaking to us, telling us about our spiritual self in the form of the greater cosmos. Words, the stars are the words of God. And no matter which God you choose, whatever his name is, whatever your area claims is the true story of god, you are correct, but you must understand so is every other faith we know of.

God is not giving preference or attention to any of us, we must listen to him/her/it not the other way around. But those messages are not demands or commandments or any construct that gives another man power or morality over another, God is personal to you and you must answer only to yourself and your version of god, do not expect anyone to adhere to your version, they are gods too.

Lucifer to me, is simply understanding this concept.

It is understanding that the ancient people left us a message, which his suggests that they knew a lot more than we give them credit for about our atomic makeup and the greater core (kaw) universe.

St Michael Defeats Satan – Guido Rene 1635
Horus slays Set

The Equinox

We have known for some time that the equinox is a time of balance in the pagan calendar, you may not have thought about the depth of meaning to the word before. *The Equine,* which means pertaining to horses, and the ox, pertaining to the bull are in harmony, or harmonics in their celestial dance. Dance is another word well worth looking into.

In Hebrew it is karar pronounced (KawRar) cor Ra (similar to the Islamic Koran) and Kor means a body or the whole body of a text for example, the source of the word Corpse. Kor-Ra is the whole "Body of Ra"

The equinox is an astronomical event of balance, the plane that represents the Horizontal (Horse-zone-tail) line at the center (English spelling - centre) of the earth, its Equin-Taur-El, equator passes the CenTAUR (center) of The Sun.

From these words we get many others such as Century (100 Years). Centrifugal, outward force created by the spin of an object. In this context the horse is The Sun, Horus. The Earth is the bull, denoted by taur or terra.

Jupiter the other morning star.

Lucifer has a well-established connection to the *Morning-star,* in modern concept 'the morning star' is generally accepted as the planet Venus. However in early texts it is suggested that the planet Jupiter was also labelled by astrologers as the morning star, and from a 'joining the dots' point of view,

Jupiter is more likely to be the planet of Lucifer for many reasons.

Jupiter is the largest planet in our solar system, it is as some would describe it a failed star, due to its enormous size and its makeup it fell short of ignition as a star. This fits in with the fallen angel description. Failed and fallen are mildly synonymous.

Jupiter gets its name from the roman god of the sky and thunder, and importantly it is the 5th planet from The Sun. The roman numeral V is representative of the number five and is seen on the illustration of the symbol of Lucifer from the Grimoirium Verum on page 44 the yet to be fully deciphered symbol has clearly a V at the bottom, which can be took to represent five or possibly V for Venus.

Jupiter across Greek, Roman, and other civilisations had several names Latin it is Iuppiter or Iūpiter, even Lu-pitar, which can with few phonetical adjustment sounds out or even reads close to Lucifer. Lu as you know by now means Light and Pitar means stone, or possibly Pita meaning Father. *Light-Stone* is a good description of the luminary description of Lucifer as the morning star or light bringer, when referred to as a planet.

Jupiter in genitive case is known as Lovis, (Jove) and in roman mythology Jove is King of the Gods and God of the sky, much like Horus in his Egyptian equivalent likewise Jupiter also shares the eagle symbology, Horus, Jorus, Lovis There are phonetic similarities to the names. The Greek Equivalent to the Roman Jupiter is Zeus. Zeus Helios Zeus, He-Zeus, Jesus, Horus, Jorus, Lovis, it really is that close and obvious a connection.

Jove in depictions is symbolised with a thunder bolt or an eagle, and quite often with both. Horus too along with his father Osiris embody the Zoroastrian eagle symbology.

Jupiter in roman mythology is twin brother of the goddess Juno, she is a mother character which we name the month of June after often appeared sitting pictured with a peacock (see *Peacock Angel*). This mother figure mentioned in all religions including Etruscan and mentioned earlier in the Lilith section had a counterpart known as Uni (Uni is latin for one O-ne) a primary creator. Uni, who is depicted on the Pyrgi Tablets is with breasts out in a typical mother and lactation symbolism feeding the adult Hercle before he 'ascends' into immortality.

However brother'ed in the caesarean calendar is the summer month of July which it is proposed and widely accepted was named after the roman emperor Julius Caesar.

Historically both Roman emperors and Egyptian pharaohs although mortal were considered by their subjects to officially be gods.

This seems a very primitive concept and yet as recently as the two thousand years ago, since the birth of the physical man we now call Jesus Christ or King of the Jews. A man who I have no doubt really existed, although I believe he was not anything more than a leader, king or prophet, attributed with the legendary attributes of the gods or sons of the gods, he was certainly not the miraculous son of a theological all powerful god, any more than the rest of us, traditionally these kings were people who were assigned the attributes of the gods and thus the mythology gains a credence of history because history will record these people.

Julius Caesar was in Roman diplomatic hierarchy a god, and just like Jesus he would have been assigned some of the traits of such a god, or son of a god.

With this I am alleging that some of the legend attributed to Julius Caesar (JC) and Jesus Christ (JC) were imbued with legends that mythology has tied to the Horus archetype. Not only that, but also it is not the case that July was named after Julius Caesar, but instead, Julius Caesar was named after Jupiter. Ju(lu) (Lu-Lius), Hulios and Helois.

Caesar was inaugurated has the high priest of Jupiter and his legend states that he was surrounded by sixty men. There are sixty minutes to the hour, hour as I have suggested is the arc of Horus, 15 degrees. (360/24=15) Julius Caesar was killed and warned "Beware the ides of March", the ides of March is the 15th of March. It is not known when Jesus is purported to have died by exact date, but is generally considered by those attempting to calculate it, anytime between April 12th and March 31st. A similar time.

Gaius Cassius Longinus, brother in law of Brutus is reputed to have led the attack that assassinated Julius Ceasar, Longinus is also the name of the roman soldier who stabbed Jesus with the spear of destiny. Jesus was betrayed by Judas, Ceasar was betrayed by Brutus whose middle name was Junius. Caesar is recorded as having been stabbed 23 times, the 23rd of July is the last day of the astrological sign of Cancer.

Baal,Beezebub,Satan the Ram.

The Caduceus symbol as mentioned above is particularly associated with Hermes in Greek mythology and in 1910 William Hayes Ward discovered that symbols similar to the classical caduceus sometimes appeared on Mesopotamian cylinder seals that dated from 4,000 to 3,000 BC. The simplified version of this rod as a glyph is presented (left) which you may recognise as the astrological symbol for Taurus or the planetary symbol for Mercury, incidentally The Roman god Mercury is associated with the Greek god Hermes.

This short explanation of the precession of the galaxies also featured in more detail in ***Exploring the Divine,*** but in case you have missed that I shall repeat a couple of sentences to bring you up to speed.

On the cosmic level, we know of the primary twelve constellations cut across the zodiac. These make up the natural zodiac; they do not appear to move, and they always remain in the same place around the zodiac *from an earth-centric point of view (as seen by the observer for you physicists).

However, because of a particular movement of the Earth's pole, The Sun crosses the Equator at a slightly different point every year. With the passing years, this point shifts by one degree approximately every 'Seventy-Two' years and as a result of this shifts signs approximately every 2,156 years. This movement is called the precession of the equinoxes. A complete cycle lasts around 25,868 years. At the end of each cycle, there is complete synchronisation between each sign and each constellation.

This two thousand, one hundred and fifty-six years is an approximation of the current zodialogical phase we are currently traveling through and the twenty-five thousand plus years approximates us passing through each of these zodialogical ages until we have cycled a full zodialogical year when like all things in nature we start again.

For simplicity I will round the number off to 2,000 years and for the past 2,000 years we have been in the zodialogical age of Pisces the fish (Christianity, the fisher of men) and so our religions feature that particular zymology, we are about or have just edged into the age of Aquarius and that will bring about a great spiritual schism, and hopefully we desire a betterment of mankind as always.

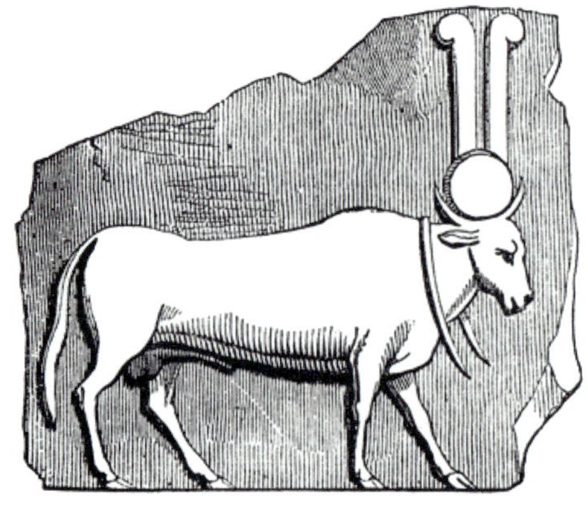

However, the reason I bring this up is to point out that the previous zodialogical age was that of Taurus, The Bull.

The schism we are about to embark upon also happened 2,000ish years ago with the transition from the worship of the Bull (Taurus, Baal, Apis or Enlil) into the worship of the Fish (Pisces, Dagon). The believers of the old ways upon the schism into Pisces primarily worshipped the bull as an iconography of our connection to God. Left is Apis (the Egyptian version of Baal), Taurus.

You may have heard of Baal as a demon in Christian mythology, in truth Baal simply means 'god' or more specifically 'lord', for instance in the case of another well-known demon Beelzebub, was originally named Baal-Zebub which means 'Lord-Flies' and so the lord of the flies, again is another adopted name for the devil in modern circles, but I believe this is actually not said in respect of an evil deity but more a mock of the old redundant god Taurus.

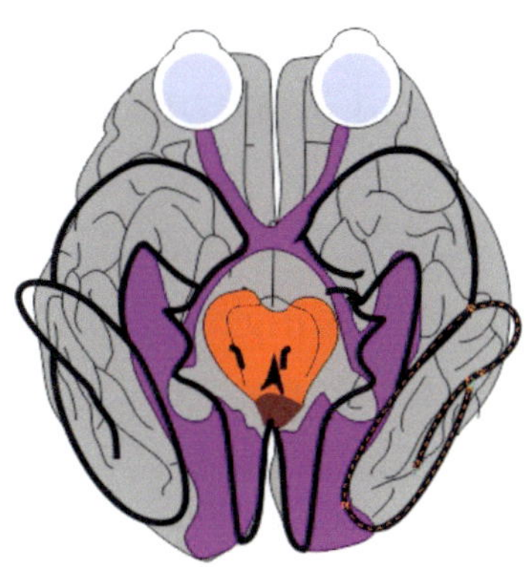

Aries the Ram

Baal is represented by a bull so what both we and the earlier religious scholars during the age of Aries the Ram(2000-33BC) would refer to it as being a Philistinic deity, because the worshipers of the bull's astrological period in its zodialogical reign was approximately 4,000 to 2,000 BC. Obviously this would then be against contemporary worship and so to worship an old god would be sacrilege to the new god (Pisces or Dagon), much like the symbolic goat being demonised as Aries the Ram, and Baal the bull is also considered a form of devil or demon worship. Baal was known as the lord with two horns. Being dated to that period of 4,000BC it ties in with very critical timeline in man's development as has been believed that this is the approximate time when man first became what we could call an industrial civilisation, prior to that he was primal hunter gatherer with basic agricultural skills but had no civil organisation other than tribal, rudimentary speech and as yet unable to build structures or conceptual architecture more substantial than rudimentary covering. It was in the area known as Mesopotamia that experts have long claimed the first cities began to form, but increasingly we are making new discoveries that defy our classic interpretation of man's development, artefacts that predate this concept are rapidly becoming the norm instead of curiosities and mysteries.

To simply put it, all the gods are one God and all the devils are old gods who have gone out of fashion. If Baal was now considered a dead god due to the introduction of Aries followed by Pisces worship then imagery of a dead bull in the desert brings about the idea of a carcass surrounded by flies and so a mockery of the 'Lord' would be to call him Lord of the flies. Baal-Zebub.

In Matthew 12:25-28 there is a reference to Beelzebub:-

> *Jesus knew their thoughts and said to them, every kingdom divided against itself will be ruined, and every city or household divided against itself will not stand. If Satan drives out Satan, he is divided against himself. How then can his kingdom stand? And if I drive out demons by Beelzebub, by whom do your people drive them out? So then, they will be your judges. But if I drive out demons by the Spirit of God, then the kingdom of God has come upon you.—*

In this passage, Jesus is appealing for unity between the old ways, and the new. Remember Satan means the Enemy(adversary), not the Devil and Beelzebub is the old lord.

Horus

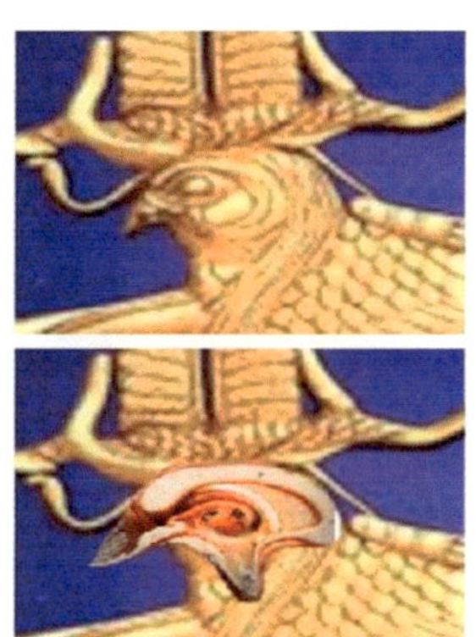

Here we have the eye of Horus, The pineal gland also mapped out over this piece of Egyptian art depicting Horus, you will also take note of the elongated columns above his head

And then we have an overlaid Bull skull with the cutaway of the brain revealing the top view of the pineal gland. Taurus, meets Horus, bulls being also a symbol of fertility and masculinity.

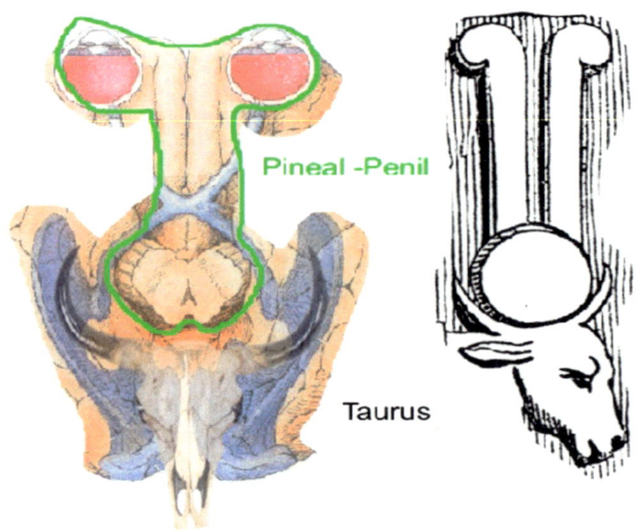

In ***Exploring the Divine*** I referenced several links establishing that the Christian Jesus is another name for the Egyptian Horus. And now Horus is also another reference to Taurus, and finally tie in the whole thing, the Hebrew version of Lucifer הֵילֵל בֶּן-שָׁחַר (Helel ben Shaḥar) means day-star, or son of the morning. This does not mean the person Jesus did not exist 2,000ish years ago, it simply means that stories once attributed to Horus and many, many other preceding deities were assigned to the person who we know as Jesus.

Ironically, if you meet most non-Christo-Luciferians and discussed Jesus they would mock, likewise a Christian would be horrified at the thought that they are a Luciferian, or that the symbolism of the Goat head representing the ram as often portrayed in a downward pointing pentagram is what the symbol of Baal (left) was once.

Elijah and the Priests of Baal by Lucas Cranach the Younger, ca. 1545.

Symbols of Lucifer Quick Reference.

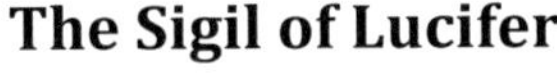

The Sigil of Lucifer

Is attributed to the sixteenth-century book known as the Grimoirium Verum, or the 'Grimoire of Truth,' the preferred keys of King Solomon. Its purpose was to bring about a visual invocation of the angel Lucifer. A version translated by Plangiere, Jesuit Dominicane is available online for free download although this symbol is not present in that version which is only 27 pages long. More comprehensive copies are available for purchase.

The Simple Pentagram

Has more of a connection to Venus than to Lucifer the archetype this ancient symbol has been adopted by almost all religious and mystical bodies over the years, astrologically speaking throughout the cycle of the year, Venus enters into a close proximity with the earth five times each at 72 degree points. Evidence that the ancients were fully aware of the earth rotating around The Sun long before Copernicus.

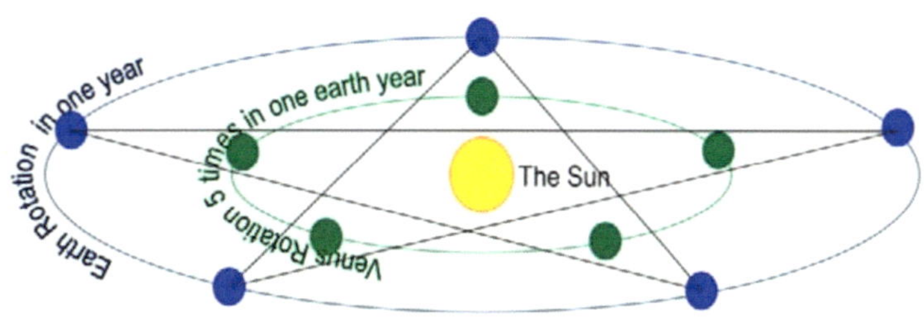

The Leviathan Cross

The Cross Satanus, draws its message from the serpent aspect of Lucifer, the cycle, the infinity symbol at its base representing the eternal cycle and renewal, crossed over represents passage from material life into the spiritual plane and a return, possibly representing re-incarnation. Chemically it represents sulphur (brimstone) and has been suggested to represent the corruption of the Christian crucifix in satanic circles although this is speculation. Origins of Leviathan Cross is believed to be in the Order of the Knights Templar.

The Gnosi-Lucif

I bear little ego, and so I reluctantly introduce this symbol as a distinction from the very elegant Sigil of Lucifer. My gnostic beliefs have been outlined in this book for your consideration and I wish this symbol to be acknowledged as a distinction from LHP Luciferianism and Satanism via the Left Hand Path, while I place great merit in its teachings I still believe that there is place for mankind to believe in a greater entity, *The Universe* as a God, who we are a biological extension of, existing within and a part of, I believe it has a collective consciousness, from which we are isolated by the mother matter. This one true god, the heart and syncretism of all gnosis and faiths. I wish this symbol to represent a spiritual awakening of man who does not hate other faiths, he embraces all and seeks the wisdom within to find a greater unification of the original divinity, *Latin: divinus 'belonging to a deity'.*

Greater Concepts of Divinity

By now, the fact you are reading this book means you have experienced the natural. I say 'experienced the natural' with a particular purpose because there exists an illusion. An illusion so powerful it consumes our entire consciousness.

We associate illusions with magic tricks and wizards and if you have ever seen a fantasy film you will have seen illusions contained within these films, films of pure fantasy. The portrayal of an illusion within this context makes the mind conceive an illusion as a fantasy themed object or an object of the imagination rather than a consequential object in the material world.

Well isn't that exactly what an Illusion would want you to think? The one thing that would reinforce illusion is the belief that there is no such thing as true illusions.

Anything you firmly believe to be true cannot possibly be an illusion from your subjective point of view because physical illusions do not exist. You firmly believe that, therefore it is true.

Now going back to my original point 'experiencing the natural'. Would it follow that if you were to encounter anything supernatural, but let's say for the sake of theoretical debate that this supernatural event was in fact a real event. Wouldn't the deceptive reality illusion that you are already immersed be inclined to tell you that the one true nature is in fact 'supernatural' and, therefore, it is not to be trusted?

I have not experienced in my life anything that some may call supernatural such as ghosts, UFO's, Yeti's you name it. I have experienced some events that others may well put down to UFO's and ghosts and the likes but my engineering-ly wired mind adopts the more scientific approach by default and always rationalises things into a context that I can either explain the phenomena to suitably satisfy myself, or as time passes I start to doubt my recollection of the event, to the point I conclude that perhaps it must simply have been my imagination or inaccurate recall.

However one thing I am convinced of is a universal source of divine power that is the alpha and omega of our consciousness, that was not just the creator of all things, but all things are a part of this great entity for which no other word fits than God.

I covered this in the chapter called ***"The eternal torment of being god".***

We have a dormant receptor in the middle of our brains which is photoreceptive, in the animals that still have this gland active it is responsible for Circadian rhythm. The Circadian rhythm is responsible for our biological timing, our sequencing of events, our sense of the passage of time, automatic functions, heart rate, sense of sleeping periods, day and night and on an atomic level physical makeup of our wavelength, frequency in relationship to our surroundings and that's the important bit.

In 1932, a scientist by the name of Louis de Broglie produced a paper suggesting that the wave-particle duality applied to not only light but to matter also.

Simply put to us laymen light had always been considered a wave. However, waves need a medium in which to pass through such as air, glass, water. The problem is though we know space is a vacuum which means it does not contain a medium for light to pass through, and yet the light from the stars and our sun, do reach the earth.

Because light traveling through the vacuum of space had no medium this simplistic view of light purely being a wave defied its own physical understanding, so the wave theory was replaced by a light particle theory.

The difference is simple waves are much like waves created when you throw a rock into a still pond, the energy transferred from the motion of the rock to find rest, hits the water, pushes the water out of its way, the water moves outwards to make way for the rock, this causes a ripple effect as the tiny molecules of water push each other away from the rock in a form of momentum. And that is why a wave requires a medium, it needs to push the energy into other receptive surroundings. Sound is such a wave, someone speaks by creating vibrations in the air, the sound vibrates in all directions outward, until it hits your eardrum which vibrates and mimics the exact same vibrations into you head where you interpret the sound. However it is inefficient, if you imagine all the energy that expands out from that point, but only one tiny bit of the wave hits your eardrum, all the rest float off until they either no longer have enough energy to vibrate their neighbour or they are absorbed by some object.

There is micro radiation that is on the shortwave radio scale but as all energy is formed of waves or particles, it exist on an optical scale depending on what you perceive to be an optical wavelength, a perception which is determined by your wavelength receptors, in our case currently the eyes.

But if the third eye which is now dormant, was such an optical receptor of such waves, with the ability, much like our eyes to interpret that data in a way our brains can make use of, it would logically reveal information that exists in our environment that we currently find difficult to perceive actually exists. We know it's there. However, it is obfuscated by our lack of ability to receive or interpret it.

This is scientific; it is not fairy stories even if it does come with a big 'IF'. The thing about magic is, all things are magic until we either fully understand how they work or observe them regularly enough that we become complacent with their occurrence. For example, we may look at The Moon every night on a clear sky, and find it majestic, beautiful, any emotion you like really, but we accept it as a natural phenomenon. Which doesn't grab too much attention? Now, if we had a second visible moon much like the one we have now but maybe in blue, covered in water and it just appeared one day, would that not be wonderful, majestic, magical, an oddity something of a wonder? Yes, of course it would, we would be dumbstruck in awe of its majesty because we could not understand it, and neither would we have sufficiently observed it. However, if that self-same moon appeared one hundred thousand years ago, our short lifespan and recorded history would accept it as normal, delightful but normal. We would probably have some theological stories explaining the wonderful, magical appearance of a new water god, scientist would be trying to discover when it arrived, where it came from, how it formed, but all this would be normal and non-magical.

In the same way, we have accepted our inability to interpret visually the data, which by another detection mechanism displays quite clearly the creation of the universe and all the stars within it. We would see this data much like we see stars with our eyes, they would be anomalies, but natural.

Edmund Bertschinger, a theoretical astrophysicist at MIT (*Massachusetts Institute of Technology*), says, 'Imagine that our eyes could detect microwave radiation, like that produced by microwave ovens. The night sky would be luminous.', what I am suggesting is that in the same way our eyes correctly interpret the abundance of seemingly random light waves and particles every day, bouncing off objects, reflections, refractions and direct light emissions into an organised view of this radiation then it is entirely possible that the Pineal gland did exactly the same with microwave radiation that would allow us to see the true view of the universe or at least a dimension of the universe that we know exists but cannot naturally see.

What prevents us from accepting this possibility is purely human arrogance, we assume that we have all the senses required to perceive all knowledge, yet we wonder how bees communicate, how flocks of birds follow migration patterns, turn in unison and a million other things creatures are able to do, that we are not. Even though we know they exist, such things as the sense of smell that a dog has being far superior to ours, the way the dog interprets the smells around it, must be as visible as a path of colour to our eyes, like Hansel and Gretel leaving breadcrumbs through the woods a dog can perceive a scent in a directional path whereas we faintly are aware of a smell in an area, the dog will turn right at a particular tree, rather than just heading in the direction of the source of the smell. It is clear that we should disregard our concepts that we are so informed by our limited senses. We are blind.

We then add to our arrogance by denying the concepts of senses out with our own. If I was to declare myself a psychic, who talks with dead people. You would be well within your rights to smile knowingly and think 'this guys a nut,' I would myself if you said the same to me, but that is my arrogance. That is me assuming that my senses are complete. Even though, I know for a fact they are not.

As a gnostic Luciferian, my belief in connecting to the universe as the full expression of interacting with our larger self is not dissimilar to Kabbalistic concepts

There is an unknowable God, that is not an abstract entity to yourself. As the greater all knowing entity we created a universe for ourselves which disconnect us from the absolution of being all things experiencing all time so that we can experience the joy of discovery. At this stage I do not want to go into the *tree of life* symbol that is always presented with the Kabbala as it strays an already strayed book away from the concept of Lucifer, but I would like to mention the structural concept of our connection to the divine universe.

Kabbalah (Kaw Baal Ah).

In Kabbalism, the unknowable God is just such an entity, which separates us by the five spiritual worlds that represent the higher concepts of thought.

Adom Kadmon, is the utmost spiritual world, our fist separation from God. It is the divine intent, the will that we should be separate and unable to share in the collective knowledge. This is achieved by the confinement to the material plane, our individual consciousness is imprisoned in the laws of materialism in its philosophical context that consciousness is a component of the material and while it is a component of it we are identified even to ourselves as being a material existence.

If we return briefly to Genesis, if mankind is the image of God then he is God, but the separation from the divine entity must have a boundary to distinguish segregation.

The spiritual form of man when re-joined to the universal collective consciousness is above individual consciousness; it is the intelligence that functions abstract from ourselves, and the first boundary is simply being a man in his spiritual nature, not his physical nature. The first man was Adam (Adom) or to add man, 'to manifest' physical form; the ball of the Atom.

Now let me explain my concept of the abstract intelligence. If faith flies in the face of science then, it is open to question, but if you can fit faith around a science model, and it surely still seems reasonable, we then can avoid the trappings of conflict and then the science supports the faith and the faith supports the science.

The unknown intellect that drives us is more likely that the automated responses that drive our hearts to beat, which can be put down to instinct or cyclic automation. The unknown intellect contained within every man or creature to me is that which drives evolution. When a butterfly evolves spots on its wings that make it look like they are big eyes, which in turn frighten away the bird, that in all likelihood would have otherwise have eaten it. Then you simply must consider that the butterfly, not within the notion of its mind nor its ancestors ever made this conscious decision to look like the face of a larger more threatening creature.

The brain of the butterfly on a local intellectual level is surely smaller and less developed than even the birds. Surely the butterfly's tiny brain in ancient times prior to this evolutionary change could not have driven this concept of survival by any internal consciousness. We did not evolve two eyes to be able to judge three-dimensional distance by choice. This is divine intent and latent potential exhibited by intelligence outside of our subjective or materially collective consciousness. Yet it belongs to us.

Please visit my Facebook page

https://www.facebook.com/Divine-Publishing-601307839969821

Also available

Exploring the Divine is a compilation of examinations and theories into the great wonders of the universe and our place in it. It explores God, The creation of the universe, Demons, Angels, Black holes, Black Magic, The big bang, Origins of religion, possibility of the computer generated universe, time travel, space exploration, perception of the self and a universal consciousness.

If you are one of those people that is fascinated by the big questions of life then this book will either provide answers or give you many interesting and new ways of philosophising the great mysteries of the universe.

There is not a dull chapter and there is something for everyone with an inquisitive mind. It also offers an aspect spiritual guidance for those battling between the evidences of the modern world and reconciliation with biblical texts. The book is split into two distinct halves beginning with religion and following up with scientific theories that are not your run of the mill current thinking but whole new concepts that will provide interesting discussions for yourself and your friends all of which while not proven or supported by current thinking is equally valid and certainly not disproven.

An objective view of religion without the purpose of either converting you to a faith or supporting atheism, but redefining our understanding of the god concept in a way compatible with modern physics and the known creation of the universe. The two are not exclusive of each other.

Are God and the Devil one in the same? Good and bad, the balance, cycle and flow of universal energy, new wave thought, magic and mysticism. Word origins and meanings.

Biblical misinterpretations. A sourcebook for anyone seeking understanding. You cannot come away from this book the same person.

Teleportation, The human occupation of distant planets in others star systems all made possible using current technology, Evolution vs intelligent design.

Made in the USA
Columbia, SC
13 June 2025

59392676R00124